TEACH ME HOW

TO LOVE YOU

COMMUNICATION AND INTIMACY IN RELATIONSHIPS

The Beginnings...

TEACH ME HOW

TO LOVE YOU

COMMUNICATION AND INTIMACY IN RELATIONSHIPS

The Beginnings...

THOMAS WEEKS III

Unless otherwise indicated, all Scripture quotations are from the authorized King James Version.

Scripture quotations marked (AMP) are from the *Amplified New Testament*, © 1954, 1958, 1987, by the Lockman Foundation, or are from the *Amplified Bible*, Old Testament, © 1962, 1964, by Zondervan Publishing House.

Language definitions have been taken from BIBLESOFT'S NEW EXHAUSTIVE STRONG'S NUMBERS AND CONCORDANCE WITH EXPANDED GREEK-HEBREW DICTIONARY. Copyright © 1994 Biblesoft and International Bible Translators, Inc. All rights reserved.

TEACH ME HOW TO LOVE YOU

Bishop Thomas Weeks III
P.O. Box 60866
Washington, DC 20039
Ph: 202-832-1100 Fax: 202-832-8059
e-mail: executiveoffice@bishopw.com
www.bishopw.com

ISBN 1-880809-24-9
Printed in the United States of America
© 2003 by Thomas W. Weeks, III

Legacy Publishers International
1301 South Clinton Street
Denver, CO 80247
www.legacypublishersinternational.com

Edited by: Paula R. Bryant
Cover design by: Kirk DouPonce, UDG
DesignWorks www.udgdesignworks.com

5 6 7 8 9 10 11 / 09 08 07 06 05 04

DEDICATION

Juanita, I dedicate this book to you, the most phenomenal woman I know. You have blessed millions of individuals; yet, in my life, you have become the greatest source of heaven outside of my personal salvation experience.

Your ability to embrace my deepest needs and to accept the challenge to invest within the potential of my God-anointed destiny, has overwhelmed my emotions with rejoicing and celebration of the integral woman that you are.

I know no one who gives more than you, prays more than you, and loves harder than you do. I am awed and thankful that God gave me the opportunity to be your husband, and you to be my wife. Every day has been a quantum leap of growth in the depth of my love, for I have never loved like this before.

I meant what I said to you in Starbuck's, and I want you to understand that I'm always learning—because love must be taught. So, forever, teach me how to love you.

Love,
Wesley

CONTENTS

FOREWORD

I couldn't be more blessed to write the Foreword for this book. First, because someone I highly respect and love deeply is the author—*my husband*. Second, it's honest. And third, it's desperately needed…especially in the church. True love is under attack and Christian marriages are failing right and left because too many believers are trying to love according to the world's concept. We're too timid about what really works and what really matters when it comes to having a godly relationship.

Both Wesley and I have learned hard lessons about love in the past, so we don't take *our love* for granted. We work at it. And so should you, if you want your marriage to survive and grow. I spent almost twenty years waiting for God to bring my husband because I had learned that unwise decisions could lead to disaster and heartbreak.

Marriage is for mature people. It takes two to make it sweet and two to make it go bad. Each one of us gets out of our marriage what we put into it. *This is real.* No matter how much you go to church, how often you speak in tongues, or how many times you pray for the sick—if you're married, you have to learn how to minister to the spiritual, physical, emotional, and sensual needs of your spouse. *This is the truth.*

There's a war going on against marriages now more than ever, so we have to learn how to *keep it real*. And we must ask God to teach us how to love in a way that pleases Him. My husband and I are learning how to do this. And he's opened his heart to share this wisdom with you, hitting the major issues that keep couples from loving each other the way God desires. I believe if you'll read each chapter prayerfully, your life will never be the same.

This is also why we both made the decision to add a bonus CD that not only includes my teaching on the "Proverbs 31 Woman," but also a powerful message from Bishop entitled, "Pride Is Just Too Expensive." We know that your life will be blessed and changed by *hearing* and *reading* the Word.

You see, the enemy knows our marriages aren't just *about us*. So he's roaming around like a roaring lion seeking whom he may devour. He's moving here and there, sowing seeds that could kill the purpose of God in our marriages…if we let him. Just remember, as a Christian, you married an eternal assignment—*not perfection*. God has entrusted you to release the potential in His son or daughter to achieve powerful things in this life and in His kingdom.

I'm so blessed that God has given me a man of the Word. And every day, I try to please and support my husband, bringing out the best God has already deposited in him. This is our commitment. This is a true marriage. This is the kind of marriage that will overcome the enemy every time.

As Wesley says, "It's time to get real." Let God expose and heal your hurts, so that you can learn how to love *His way*.
—Juanita Bynum

INTRODUCTION

One Saturday afternoon (following a wonderful Friday evening date at the theater), Juanita and I experienced our first conversational difficulty (better known to others as an argument). We both had such different views of the situation that we couldn't bring it to terms. Finally, after much "heated fellowship," we decided to meet at Starbuck's and discuss a way to solve the issue.

I was pretty tense and nervous while waiting for her to arrive; yet, I was confident that God had called me to be her husband. And I understood that *I* would need to make the sacrifice at this meeting, not her. However, when Juanita stepped out of her car, she took ten steps toward me and opened her arms. I walked to her and we embraced. At that moment, I knew even more surely that there was a covenant between us that needed to be kept and nurtured.

We went into Starbuck's, ordered two of our favorite drinks, and began to dialogue about what we felt was wrong at that point in our relationship. Interestingly, the sensitive things she shared only confirmed what had already been in my spirit about how I truly needed to love her. And I recognized that inside of the great prophetess everybody knew—deep in her innermost being—was a woman who just wanted to be loved for her-self...Juanita.

As tears began to run down her cheeks, I moved in close, grabbed her hands, and placed them on my chest as if to say, "Feel me; I know where you're at." Then I looked deep in her eyes and said, "Teach me how to love you."

There's a really great thing about relationships. A man can give a woman candy, flowers, money, a house, a car, or a vaca-tion...but what she really wants is *intangible*. A woman wants a man to grow and love her the way she needs to be loved. And though I had the capacity to love Juanita in a godly way, my compassion could be unlocked only after I was able to *hear her*. Only then could I take that truth and love her from the depth of her need.

As a man, I had to be open to hear Juanita's *need to love*, so that I could develop the capacity to lead her *through love*.

While we were still at the table, she turned and reached deep inside of my spirit, ministering to a part of me that hadn't been touched for years. My issues had been buried deep be-neath the surface, under all the things I'd been—minister, son, bishop, grandson, anointed man of God, pastor, preacher, and so on. My pain was hidden under everything I was to every-body else. Yet, that day, Juanita touched my needs that had been shattered, scarred, and buried under the scaffolding of ministry.

As she poured into my heart, it made me recognize that she was teachable...because she saw my pain, felt my need, and understood my potential. Before it was over, Juanita and I had formed a bond that's now the foundation of our marriage.

Since that time, we've sensed a strong leading of the Lord to share with others what we've learned about building a godly relationship. So along with this book, Juanita has included a powerful teaching on the "Proverbs 31 Woman," and I've added an in-depth message dealing with pride—both on the same bonus CD. We're trusting God that you'll be strengthened and inspired.

All in all, you'll get a glance at our relationship along with powerful teachings that will bless your life. And hear me: *This book is honest.* So whether you're a man or a woman, you'll be confronted by the truth—because, friend, it's time for Christians to get real about relationships. You'll be challenged, whether you're *in a marriage* or waiting *for a marriage.* We also believe it will give you hope, knowing that somebody else has come through situations you may still be dealing with. *Hear me:* God will give you victory in your relationship if you'll embrace wisdom and be honest about who you are.

After this book, we'll be releasing two more volumes in the *Teach Me How to Love You* series. We're writing the next book, *Forever Us,* together. This volume will minister from the deeper commitment God is bringing in our marriage. And finally, our third volume on *The Family* will share from our experiences of building a legacy for the future.

God loves you so much that He'll process your life both *for* a godly marriage and *in* your marriage. Our prayer is that you'll be blessed with true love and glean the need to be taught how to love—because love isn't conclusive. Love isn't final. *Love is a process, and it must be taught.*

As you learn from the principles I've shared in this volume, may you begin to say in your heart, *Teach Me How to Love You.*

I

In the Beginning... The Wisdom of God

God's Wisdom for Establishing a Godly Relationship

> From the time I first met her, Juanita shone
> with the glory of God. She captivated me. It didn't take long
> before I knew she would be my wife.
> —TWW

- Emerging from a painful past into a new season of destiny
- Overcoming spiritual paralysis from old issues and insecurities
- Learning what makes men and women tick

*A capable, intelligent, and virtuous woman—who
is he who can find her?*
Proverbs 31:10 AMP

CHAPTER 1

A WASHING OF WISDOM

The fear of the Lord is the beginning of knowledge:
but fools despise wisdom and instruction.
Proverbs 1:7

The process of wisdom can be an interesting paradox. Many times it humbles you to wash away the past and build God's character in you for the future. This was definitely true for Juanita and me. We both came through seasons of stripping before we met. During those times of divine processing, we each learned that our first, most vital relationship is with God. And from this relationship, all others would be birthed as we obeyed His voice.

Thinking back several years to my own experience, I had gone from being married and enjoying a successful life to being alone with barely enough to survive. For two years, I went through a painful process in which God tested my commitment to His will. I lost everything, even friends in the ministry. People stopped inviting me to preach and every door seemed to be slamming in my face. That's when I learned to give all my praises to God. That's when I embraced wisdom. And that's when God birthed a new vision in me.

My wife's experience was different, yet just as devastating. She loved the Lord, but she had made a bad relationship choice that eventually brought her to the point of trying to take her own life. That's when God spoke to her. He told her to fulfill her marriage vows...and she embraced wisdom. She remained faithful to her commitment until the day her husband said, "It's time for me to go." He gave her the keys and never came back.

Juanita walked through many dark times until the Lord brought her through to victory. Then one day while writing her book, *No More Sheets*, God spoke to her in a still, soft voice and said, "The eclipse is over!" This revelation still blesses me today:

A solar eclipse occurs when the sun seems to vanish....The moon comes between the Earth and the sun, briefly hiding the sun and casting a shadow on the Earth. But, it only lasts for a few minutes. Now let's look at the revelation of this. Many times, there have been things in our lives that have passed between God and us....The moon gets its light from the sun.... There is no water on the moon, which means there is nothing to fulfill a thirst and it has no atmosphere, so it cannot support life....Think about how the enemy works when he brings a relationship into your life that is not the will of the Lord. One of the ways to judge whether or not you are about to experience a solar eclipse is this: There is no atmosphere, which means there is no presence of the Lord there. There is no life—meaning the life of the Lord—flowing out of that individual into you or out of you into that individual...[1]

Juanita goes on to teach that nothing can be built or formed where there is no atmosphere, so the relationship will always be rocky. Zero gravity (like on the moon) means that nothing about this relationship will keep you steady and hold you firmly on the ground. The sun, on the other hand, generates energy that spreads light and heat, allowing life to exist on Earth. So when an eclipse occurs and the moon comes between you and the Son—your source of power and light—the life of God can't grow there. This is a powerful revelation, and we've both walked through it. We have endured the processing.

An eclipse is a paradox, *just like wisdom*. Light fades and darkness falls for a moment...but the Son is shining just behind that lifeless situation. And if you keep your eyes on Him, He'll wash away the darkness in the morning!

Wisdom washed us, and it can wash you—no matter what kind of relationship problems you've been dealing with. A bad relationship experience got Joseph thrown into prison, but the Lord blessed him there (Genesis 39:7–23). He emerged from darkness by interpreting Pharaoh's dream. Then Pharaoh told Joseph, *"Forasmuch as God hath shewed thee all this, there is none so discreet and wise as thou art"* (Genesis 41:39). Joseph was instantly promoted to a position of power and authority (Genesis 41:45).

Wisdom washed Jacob when he was alone near the brook of Jabbok (Genesis 32:22–30). He wrestled against a mysterious man the whole night, and when the sun rose again, he had passed from the old into the new.

> *And he said, Thy name shall be called no more Jacob,*
> *but Israel: for as a prince hast thou power with God*
> *and with men, and hast prevailed. And Jacob asked*

him, and said, Tell me, I pray thee, thy name. And he said, Wherefore is it that thou dost ask after my name? And he blessed him there. And Jacob called the name of the place Peniel: for I have seen God face to face, and my life is preserved (Genesis 32:28–30).

Wisdom can wash your situation. It can bless you in the place of your struggle and preserve your destiny. You can get victory in relationships. You just have to go deeper in God—*see His face*—and endure His season of processing by obeying whatever He reveals to your spirit. This tells God whether or not He can trust you with what *you believe* He has for your life.

Our New Season Begins

People often ask me how I ended up marrying Juanita Bynum. My answer is always the same: *God could trust my heart.* And He captured my heart signal by challenging me in giving. The gift I sowed in obedience to the Lord confirmed that He could trust me—and not just with my own resources, but also with another vessel in His kingdom. I'm more convinced than ever that God ordained our relationship and purposed it to be birthed from my obedience.

I still remember that day in February 2002. I had been on the road for about six hours when God told me to drive to Atlantic City, New Jersey, where Juanita was holding church revival meetings at Victory Deliverance Temple. Out of habit, I called my driver, but he wasn't available. Then the Lord reprimanded me, "I told you to go alone." So I jumped back into my car around 6:00 p.m., programmed the church's address into the navigation system, and headed off in traffic from Washington, D.C. to Atlantic City.

The Holy Ghost said, "When you get there, sow a $1,000 seed." "Okay, God," I responded. "Whenever You tell me to give a $1,000 seed, I know that You're going to turn something for me." While I was driving, the revelation of that seed sank deep into my spirit and the Lord began to show me four things. All of them came to pass.

First, I knew while I was walking down the aisle of her meeting she'd ask to see me after the service. Second, I was supposed to ask her to speak at our church. Third, I would invite her to speak at our annual Destiny Conference, and fourth, there were going to be flashing lights behind my car. Each of these things came to my spirit while driving between Washington, D.C. and Laurel, Maryland.

When I reached the Atlantic City Expressway, about thirty-four miles outside the city, flashing lights appeared and I was pulled over by a police officer. Remembering the revelation, I said to him, "Guess what? I'm going to tell you the truth. I was doing about eighty-two miles per hour…I'm on my way to a move of God in Atlantic City at Victory Deliverance Temple." He looked at me, asked for my vehicle registration, and then came back *and only issued me a warning.*

Then he surprised me by asking if I knew where the meeting was located—because he was going to take me there!

Let's pause here. When God has destined something for your life, He'll make sure He lines you up for it to happen. As a matter of fact, the thing that looks like it's supposed to stop you and paralyze your progress will actually be what gets you where God wants you to be *right on time.* My navigation system had indicated I'd be arriving at the church between 9:19 p.m. and 9:30 p.m. Even with getting pulled over, I arrived right at 9:19 p.m. *with a police escort.*

At first, I was worried that I was going to miss the offering because I'd been pulled over, but God said, "No, I'm going to make it come to pass." *Sometimes God challenges your faith.* I was definitely challenged that night—but He rewarded my obedience. Today, the love of my life is my wife because I obeyed the Holy Ghost and drove hundreds of miles at the last minute to give a sacrificial offering.

As a prophet, I have to give you the truth of His Word. When you draw close to the Lord and obey Him, He'll bless your life according to what He's destined for you to become. So when I look back on my early years, I'm not ashamed of what I went through to become who I am today. I had to go through dark times so that God could trust me to be honest with you about my life and His Word. Yes, my early season of processing was painful. No, I wouldn't want to go through it again...but I'm glad that I did. And I'm a much better man today than I was twelve or thirteen years ago.

Let me encourage you. Never think God won't use your bad experiences to bless your future. If you learn from them, that's ninety percent of what He'll use to help you succeed.

My greatest miracle came when God challenged me during my greatest time of suffering. You see, God wants to bless your life—but He has to be able to trust you. This means you must do what He's already given you the ability to do *right now.* And remember, God never asks you to give up something unless He's already prepared something to take its place.

Are you ready for God to bless your relationship? Then you must be willing for Him to process you. God already understands that old things must pass away, and He'll challenge you in order to move them out of your way. So you have to seek His face and rise to a new level by obeying whatever God reveals for you to do. If you're single, you'll need a washing of wisdom for marriage. And if you're married, you'll need to be washed daily to keep your love alive.

> *Wisdom is the principal thing; therefore get wisdom: and with all thy getting get understanding. Exalt her, and she shall promote thee: she shall bring thee to honour, when thou dost embrace her. She shall give to thine head an ornament of grace: a crown of glory shall she deliver to thee* (Proverbs 4:7–9).

From Revelation to Anointing

God will always accomplish His purpose in your life through His Spirit. This means you have to process God's revelation before you receive the anointing to live in it. Joseph had a dream that revealed he would ultimately rule over his brothers. Then he went through the processing. Jacob was destined to become Israel, but God had to process him before he could be trusted with his inheritance.

God is going to challenge you to grow in wisdom—especially in situations that have been hard for you to face—because if you don't grow in those areas, He can't trust you with His blessings. Recently, the Lord stopped me and said, "I'm not going to give out false miracles. I'm not going to give out blessings merely because somebody's praising Me.

I'm giving them out now because I can trust that person to be a foundation of truth."

We are in a season where God is allowing His people to tap into a realm of purification in our spirits. This means you have to become a person of "hearing." According to Proverbs 1:5, *"A wise man will hear, and will increase learning; and a man of understanding shall attain unto wise counsels."* You must hear so that you can become instructed of God, and this counsel will cause you to develop skills that edify your life and relationships.

The problem is, too many Christians have no communion with God yet want Him to bless their relationships with others. They are always asking for a word, seeking for somebody else's prayers, and looking for the easy way out of their problems. *In short, they don't want to go through the process.* They don't want to process through the sacrifice of obedience that brings rich rewards.

God can wash you in wisdom by giving you information, revelation, and impartation. Let me explain. Information informs you. Revelation allows you to discern the information on a deeper level. Impartation gives you the capacity to carry the revelation. In other words, information develops the capacity to receive revelation, which sets the groundwork for divine impartation.

How often do you read your Bible on a weekly basis? If you never read it, how can you expect to get a revelation of who God is? And if He can't get information and knowledge into your spirit, you'll never get revelation. Hosea 4:6 says, *"My people are destroyed for lack of knowledge...."* So when you get knowledge, God can turn that into an opportunity to give you revelation. Then after revelation is birthed in your spirit, you can receive the impartation to obey what God has revealed and instructed you to do.

In other words, if you want God to bless your relationship, you have to seek Him first—*so that you can see His face.* Not for Him to give you a wife or a husband, or to save your marriage. *Seek God to know Him.* Then He'll help you build a godly relationship. Seek Him daily in prayer, study your Bible, and become a person of "hearing." Then the wisdom of God will begin to wash your life.

People who have wisdom don't need public opinion to move on the things of God because sound counsel is already in their spirits. They can say, "That sounds like God, and I can check it in my spirit, because the Word of God says…" Become a person of "hearing," and then God will make you a foundation for truth and things will start moving in your life.

The question is, are you willing to give up yourself to get God? The struggle isn't in knowing that God lives; it's in letting Him live in you. Instead of praying, "God, do this *for* me," we need to let Him do something *inside* of us. Are you willing to die so that Christ can live in your relationship? If so, then you can take comfort in knowing that as much as you give up for Him, He'll willingly give it back to you *and more.*

From Anointing to Authority

Let me clarify with a personal story, since we all "miss the mark" every now and then. For example, God may speak to me about something, and as much as I know His voice, I could act like I don't know Him—like the time I was on my way to the airport to meet my wife in the Bahamas. The weather was bad, there was a two-hour traffic delay, and the cutoff to check my luggage was thirty minutes before takeoff.

All the way to Reagan National, I was calling the airline's Chairman's Preferred office to find out if my flight was delayed. "No, sir…it's on time." I started praying, "God, delay the flight for me." I didn't know they were going to shut down the airport when I got to the ticket counter. And while we were driving, God kept telling me to grab my luggage; and the whole time I was arguing, "There's not enough time…"

To make a long story short, when I arrived at the airport fifteen minutes before departure, they told me the plane was boarding (even though the airport was closing). Then the person asked me, "Do you have any luggage?" Shocked and humbled, I said, "No, I left it in the trunk." I missed the mark. I didn't obey Him.

You see, when God sets you up for favor, you don't have any excuses. Time isn't a factor! Instead of listening to God, I was thinking about all the Sky Caps I knew (whose numbers I didn't have programmed in my phone). I was planning to tell whoever I could contact, "Print my ticket, make sure I have everything I need, so as soon as I pull up, I can throw you my luggage and run to catch the plane…" Then when I got to the ticket counter, the last person I expected to ask, "Where's your luggage?" wanted to know how many pieces I had to check. Stupefied, I said, "I don't have any."

To make matters worse, I hadn't carried my luggage because I didn't think I'd have anybody to give it to in case I couldn't check it on the flight—because I was arguing with God. However, when I arrived, I immediately saw a very good friend (who normally works at another airport) whose brother is a Bishop in our organization. She was working right next to the person handling the First Class section. I've known her for more than twenty years, so if it had turned out that I couldn't check my luggage, I could have easily told her, "Hold on to this until someone from my office comes to pick it up." God had a backup for me—but I missed the opportunity.

Last year, I took 162 flights. As of this writing, I've already been on 40 planes. *I just knew* they wouldn't take my luggage...so I argued with God because I didn't want to be embarrassed. I was trying to avoid the drama at the counter. *I was trying to protect me.* Then to make matters even worse, when I got to the gate, the person asked, "Do you have any luggage?" Beside myself, I said, "Can you give me ten minutes? I'll be right back." She replied, "No, we don't have ten minutes. You have to get on the plane now, because the airport has just re-opened."

Lo and behold, I boarded the airplane...and it didn't take off for another hour. That burned me up! So for a whole hour I sat on the plane thinking, *I could have had my luggage.* And I repented the whole time. I wanted God to know that I was truly sorry for not trusting Him and doing what He had told me to do.

When I arrived in the Bahamas, I had to wear the same clothes for a day and a half until my other clothes arrived by Federal Express. I paid $211 and some change to get a little box—because I wasn't obedient to God's voice. Hear me. Disobedience will cost you. You see, God challenged me with a non-spiritual issue. He didn't challenge me with how much I prayed, read my Bible, or spoke in tongues. He didn't challenge me about the message I was going to preach. My challenge was, "Are you going to carry your luggage?"

The next time I had a similar situation at the airport, I obeyed God and made the flight—luggage and all. That's when He told me, "If you learn how to speak with authority that I give favor in your life, it will happen." Bad situations can make you fearful. Your own reasoning can make you miss the mark if you're not a person of "hearing." In that situation, I just didn't want to miss the plane. I hadn't seen my wife for four days, so to me, the luggage could wait. I was anxious, thinking I could buy what I needed when I got there. I wasn't hearing and obeying God's voice.

So you see, my struggle isn't smoking, drinking, or gambling. My struggle is being obedient because of the information, revelation, and impartation that I'm trusting God to release into my life. I have to trust Him when everything else says, "Absolutely not!" When God tells me He's going to do something special, I can void my own blessing if I fail to obey. Hear me. Disobedience ultimately ends in pain. And the pain is, *I should have known better*.

Let God Process You

Sometimes we excuse away the processing of God because we have alternatives. I can tell you from my own experience that you need to receive God's processing in your life. It can make the difference between marriage and divorce, or even life and death. My wife and I have learned this lesson well.

God tests and processes every area of your life. Sometimes you'll know He's speaking to you—but you sit there and act like it's a non-issue *because you know what you know*. Let me help you. When God starts processing you about your wife, husband, fiancé, or friend, don't disobey His voice. You never know what God's going to set up for you. God will give you favor in extreme situations.

The Word of God has a lot to say about building a healthy, godly relationship—whether you're dating, engaged, or married. And once you get this information, you can receive revelation that will begin the process of transforming your life. Better yet, you'll be lined up for divine impartation to do what God has revealed to your spirit. My wife once said, "There's a process in, and there's a process out" of the sheets.[2] In other words, there's a way to break the bondage caused by ungodly relationships and past mistakes. Start by getting into the presence of God. Then the atmosphere will be set for growth, and life will begin to flow into your relationship.

The eclipse is over. Wisdom will wash you, if you let it.

Endnotes

1. Juanita Bynum, *No More Sheets* (Lanham, Maryland: Pneuma Life Publishing, 1998), 231–232.

2. Ibid., 41.

CHAPTER 2

THE POWER TO WALK AGAIN

...He said to the paralyzed man, I say to you, arise,
pick up your litter (stretcher), and go to your own house!
Luke 5:24 AMP

Recently, my wife shared that before we started dating, she thought all her past hurts had been healed. So when they started resurfacing, she was shocked. Juanita didn't realize the pain was still there, since she hadn't dated anyone for about fifteen years. That's when she cried out to God

Purify me...everything from the past.
Let it surface so I can see who I really am!

Of course, I was going through the same thing. I became aware of issues that were tied to my past, and I began to see the reality of how they had affected me. God really had to help me.

In short, we both underwent a whole new "washing" process. Things got real...pretty quickly. We cared for each other deeply, but God was exposing every hidden issue to bring us to the altar. He was purifying us for what was to come. Therefore, we both had to change. And we've continued to work hard at our relationship so that old hurts and insecurities won't paralyze our potential in God. We understand that our relationship has an eternal purpose.

Jesus said, *"And ye shall know the truth, and the truth shall make you free"* (John 8:32). If you want to break free from the bondage of past relationships, you have to start by *knowing the truth*. You can't avoid the process. If you're dealing with issues in your relationship, understand that God is allowing them to come to the surface. He's exposing these issues so that you'll learn how to handle them according to His Word.

As Juanita says, *no trouble, no marriage*—because God will take what the enemy uses to hurt you and turn it into a Holy Ghost testimony! (Romans 8:28) If you submit to the process, God will use your pain to take your relationship to the next level.

Don't Get Paralyzed

Let's start by reading an interesting story from Luke 5:17–25 in the Amplified Bible.

One of those days, as He was teaching, there were Pharisees and teachers of the Law sitting by, who had come from every village and town of Galilee and Judea and from Jerusalem. And the power of the Lord was [present] with Him to heal them. And behold, some men were bringing on a stretcher a man who was paralyzed, and they tried to carry him in and lay him before [Jesus]. But finding no way to bring him in because of the crowd, they went up on the roof and lowered him with his stretcher through the tiles into the midst, in front of Jesus. And when He saw [their confidence in Him, springing from] their faith, He

*said, Man, your sins are forgiven you! And the
scribes and the Pharisees began to reason and question and argue, saying, Who is this [Man] Who
speaks blasphemies? Who can forgive sins but God
alone? But Jesus, knowing their thoughts and questionings, answered them, Why do you question in
your hearts? Which is easier: to say, Your sins are
forgiven you, or to say, Arise and walk [about]? But
that you may know that the Son of Man has the
[power of] authority and right on earth to forgive
sins, He said to the paralyzed man, I say to you,
arise, pick up your litter (stretcher), and go to your
own house! And instantly [the man] stood up before
them and picked up what he had been lying on and
went away to his house, recognizing and praising and
thanking God.*

The Bible never tells us how this man became paralyzed.
Notice it didn't say he was lame, for "lame" means he never
had activity, usage, or experience with his legs. Since he once
had the ability to move, the paralysis was handicapping him
from fulfilling his purpose—and that's what happens in many
relationships. To *paralyze* means "…to bring to a condition of
helpless stoppage or inability to act."[1] Paralysis is caused either
by disease or injury.

Let's look at the revelation. When you're spiritually paralyzed, you know what your potential is, but something keeps
cutting it back. You know things could be different, but you're
stuck lying still. It means, "I know I don't belong here, but I
can't do anything about it because I don't have the power to get
up on my own." Something caused this to happen, so you need

to expose the sin (disease) and unresolved issues (injuries) by bringing them to Jesus.

Watch Out for Enticement

The enemy will fight tooth and nail to keep you in bondage. And he'll use the same deadly weapon that got you there in the first place...*enticement.* James 1:13–14 says,

> *Let no man say when he is tempted, I am tempted of God: for God cannot be tempted with evil, neither tempteth he any man: but every man is tempted, when he is drawn away of his own lust, and enticed.*

In the Greek, *enticed* means "to entrap....a trick (bait)" (Strong's, #G1185/#G1388). *Webster's American Family Dictionary* adds, "to lead on by exciting hope or desire; allure; tempt...".[2] When you're enticed, nothing ever seems to be good enough. You always feel like you need to be striving for something new or different—*and it's usually something that isn't meant for you.* Enticement is one of the primary tools of the enemy. It's a major issue that wreaks havoc in relationships, and I'll show you how.

For example, have you ever dated somebody and then a little while after breaking up, wondered how you ever dated that person? Something *enticed* you to commit to that relationship, *but it was never meant for you.* The enemy tempted you and said, "You need this person because the relationship you have isn't good enough." Then you ended up asking yourself, "How in the world did I ever get that close to that person?" If you're honest, you'll admit that you didn't really seek God about it, so sin enticed you.

When I was a young man, I was dating a certain young lady who was two years older than me. She was a very nice person. To be honest, though, I was excited about dating her because she was built nice and solid. I was only thinking about hugging, kissing, and sex. I wasn't looking for real romance, love, and marriage. I was feeling my oats.

On one of our dates, we went to see a professional baseball game and returned two days later. I'll never forget what happened. We were downstairs at my house, and I was sitting at the piano working on a few runs when my parents walked in. As they were getting ready to go back upstairs, I said, "Dad and Mom, we've got an announcement to make. I'm going to marry so-and-so." Both of them stopped, turned around, and said, "No, you're not."

There was silence in the house for a long time. I just knew I was in love! The fact is, *I was enticed.* I was enticed by what I was seeing and could have in that relationship. I was enticed by what I thought I needed. Now I know marrying her would have been a big mistake, even though she was a wonderful person.

My whole argument with my parents was, "No, you don't know. I'm in love. I've been praying for this person, I've been asking God to do it. I've been asking God to allow this relationship…" And I really was. I remember praying, "Lord, allow her to like me…" because she was an older woman. I had tried a relationship with a younger woman, and it didn't work. So I went for a more mature relationship—still, I was paralyzed. I was seeking God for a woman; *I wasn't seeking to know Him.*

When I started dating, I felt like "the man." So when my parents stopped me from doing what I wanted, I was heartbroken…devastated. Yet, they had the wisdom of God. They knew who I was *becoming*; at the time, *I didn't.* I got wind of it later.

Sin had enticed me through my desires—but hear me, you can desire something that's absolutely wrong for your future. Sister, just because somebody comes up to you and likes you—and he's never looked that tall or strong before—don't get enticed. Just because he's never spent that much time pursuing you before, don't be seduced by what looks new. He could be someone who's not going to marry you and your destiny.

Be happy when God holds you back from embracing something that entices you. It's a trick of the enemy aimed directly at your flesh. If you feed it, you won't only be paralyzed, you also could abort your destiny. Embrace wisdom. Romans 6:18–23 says,

> *Being then made free from sin, ye became the servants of righteousness. I speak after the manner of men because of the infirmity of your flesh: for as ye have yielded your members servants to uncleanness and to iniquity unto iniquity; even so now yield your members servants to righteousness unto holiness. For when ye were the servants of sin, ye were free from righteousness. What fruit had ye then in those things whereof ye are now ashamed? for the end of those things is death. But now being made free from sin, and become servants to God, ye have your fruit unto holiness, and the end everlasting life. For the wages of sin is death; but the gift of God is eternal life through Jesus Christ our Lord.*

Let me take you back a little further. Enticement came to me when I was pretty young. I remember one day when one of the older kids started showing *one of those books*. Whew! We were enticed! "Wow! Is that for real? How does *that* work?" Pornography is no joke. It's everywhere in our society, and one way or another, you've seen it. The question is, *is it enticing you?* If so, then it will make you want to entice yourself more by getting more books, looking at videos, and doing all kinds of things that embrace your sensual appetites. Eventually, enticement will change you into something you're not—because the spirit of that thing will transfer to you.

One day not long ago, I clicked on something in my email box and stuff started popping up all over the place! Nowadays, you don't have to buy pornography; it finds you! "Click here for a free vacation..." Then, suddenly, stuff starts popping up. *It's a trick to entice you.* Watch that spirit—because the enemy is trying to bait you. Do you really think you're going to find a godly relationship in a porno chat room? And if you're doing and you're married, it will tear your relationship apart.

We've got to get real...because enticement is lethal! It will actually intimidate you into thinking, *Why don't I have this on my body? Why doesn't this happen for me when I feel sexual?* Before you realize it, you'll start handling your relationship according to your enticement. You'll start viewing what you need from your spouse out of some book, versus anointed understanding that comes only from the wisdom of God.

This is why married couples have to learn how to love each other—for everything we are and everything we're not—because once you stop loving what you were *enticed* to embrace, you're going to be tempted. If you're not tapped into God's wisdom, then when something that enticed you about your spouse changes, you'll start looking for the same enticement in somebody else. Instead of going through God's process in your marriage, you'll be paralyzed.

If you're single, you need to find out why that person loves you. Act up once or twice and see how he or she reacts. Sister, is he loving you for your personality? Character? Maybe he's drawn to your physical sensuality. Brother, maybe she's attracted to your work ethic. You're really driven and motivated, and it entices her. Whatever the enticement is, if it ever changes or stops, will that person still love you? First Thessalonians 5:21–24 says,

> *Prove all things; hold fast that which is good. Abstain from all appearance of evil. And the very God of peace sanctify you wholly; and I pray God your whole spirit and soul and body be preserved blameless unto the coming of our Lord Jesus Christ. Faithful is he that calleth you, who also will do it.*

What Happened to Your Foundation?

The problem is that sin will get you around people who love to do exactly what you're being enticed to do. So you have to be careful who your friends are, for your friends prophesy your future. They point the direction you're headed. Take my advice. Don't allow people to hang around your life who don't have as much wisdom as you do. They'll start speaking things in your spirit that put acid on the values of God. Eventually, you'll have no foundation to stand on. I have seen it happen too many times.

For example, a single woman with real anointing on her life can be enticed to date somebody who's on drugs. All the while, she'll be thinking, *God's going to save him one day...* And it may be true. God may save him one day, but He doesn't need her to save him! Yet, she'll rationalize, "He needs me to save him, because he comes to me when he's down and depressed." She doesn't have the wisdom of God in this situation because God's not going to sacrifice her anointing to save him! When God wants to save somebody, He simply sends out His Spirit and draws that person.

Too often, singles can create their own delusion about "why God needs me to save this relationship...." How can you believe God has anything to do with that? How can you believe that shacking up with a man is going to save him? How is sleeping with him every other night going to bless him? What's he going to think about your God when you show up at church with him? How is God supposed to save him when He hasn't gotten you saved yet?

Still, you justify the enticement because it pleases your flesh. "Well, we're just going to live in two different rooms. You live on that side, and I'll live on this side. We'll eat breakfast together, and go out sometimes, but until we're married...cause I just know you're my husband." You're in Drama School, because you can't hear God and increase in learning while you're living a lie! A sister's sleeping with a man she's trying to save. A brother's sleeping with a woman he's trying to save...*and everybody knows what you're doing*.

You're not living what you profess, so how can you be a witness to anyone? And how can you expect God to bless you? You can't come to church and play games with God. You have to come before Him in truth. What are you going to do when hell hits your house? What are you going to do when the pressure hits your destiny? What will you do when foolishness tries to attack your faith, or when sin is trying to rob you of success?

Too many people in the church today are struggling to hear instruction because they're in bondage to *enticement*; therefore, they're not increasing in anything! If you want to go to another level in your relationship, you need to start by getting God's wisdom in your spirit. Remember Proverbs 1:7: *"The fear of the LORD is the beginning of knowledge: but fools despise wisdom and instruction."* Unless you begin to reverence "wisdom," there's going to be a struggle in your life to gain the knowledge of God. Your relationship will suffer…and your destiny will hang in the balance.

God wants you to come through His processing; He wants you to increase beyond what you've always known. Don't let enticement paralyze your life. Let God wash you, and don't look back. God has something for your future.

Rise Up and Walk Again

This takes me back to the fifth chapter of Luke:

But finding no way to bring him in because of the crowd, they went up on the roof and lowered him with his stretcher through the tiles into the midst, in front of Jesus. And when He saw [their confidence in Him, springing from] their faith, He said, Man, your sins are forgiven you! And the scribes and the Pharisees began to reason and question and argue, saying, Who is this [Man] Who speaks blasphemies? Who can forgive sins but God alone? But Jesus, knowing their thoughts and questionings, answered them, Why do you question in your hearts? Which is easier: to say, Your sins are forgiven you, or to say, Arise and walk [about]? But that you may know that the Son of Man has the [power of] authority and right on earth to forgive sins, He said to the paralyzed man, I say to you, arise, pick up your litter (stretcher), and go to your own house! And instantly [the man] stood up before them and picked up what he had been lying on and went away to his house, recognizing and praising and thanking God (Luke 5:19–25 AMP).

Now let's think about this. His friends climbed up on the roof and ripped up as much as they could to get him through it. Do you think it's likely they tore out six feet of the roof, or maybe just two or three? I probably would have ripped off as little as possible, just enough to get him inside—which means he would have gone in at an angle. *In other words, the stretcher had to become his place of safety and blessing.* It became the support that kept him from falling when he was going down.

Remember, whatever you've been struggling with can become the thing that actually gets you through to Jesus for healing. The situation that handicapped you can turn into a blessing when you bring it to Him. That's what Juanita and I have learned. *Have you been enticed?* The sin or injury that's attached you to your sickbed can save your life by ushering you safely into the presence of God.

This also reveals the character people around us need to possess because sometimes we need help to get to the altar. Sometimes other people might have to carry you. Brother, it could be your wife. Sister, it could be your husband. It could be your mother, father, best friend, or all of the above.

The men in the story are an excellent example. They let their paralyzed friend down *"into the midst."* That means Jesus was completely surrounded, yet they were strategic enough to lower the bed right in front of Him. They had the ability to view the crowd and determine exactly where Jesus was…and then remember that exact location from the roof. Not only that, but they also had to keep steady while working together. Talk about wisdom!

It's not easy to carry someone in prayer, especially if it's your spouse, because feelings are involved. My wife says it takes a real woman to birth out a man in prayer. I believe the same principle holds true for men—because when you're enticed to want what you want, it takes a process of purification for your flesh to die. Sometimes God has to deal with us to bring us to the altar.

Think about it. The men were carrying dead weight all the way to the house, and then up onto the roof. Most likely, their muscles were aching and they were dying of thirst. On top of this, each one of them probably had a few other things he could have been doing instead of lowering somebody through a roof. *One thing's for sure*: Enticement didn't have anything to do with it. This couldn't have appealed to their flesh. They trusted God and were committed to the relationship.

Do you get the revelation? If your relationship is going to endure God's process, you have to learn how to carry each other to the altar—because the greatest assignment in any marriage is this: *I'm not going to let you fail*. Tell each other, "If I ever get paralyzed, pick me up and drag me into His presence." Make sure he or she knows how to get you to God—because you can reach your potential only by seeing His face.

If you're not married, make sure the people around you love and worship God. Make sure they have a relationship with

Him that taps into revelation because when you're paralyzed, they'll be equipped to do whatever it takes to get you to the altar. And please...when you're dating, *prove all things*. Take time to know this man or woman by the spirit. Second Corinthians 5:16–17 says,

> *Wherefore henceforth know we no man after the flesh: yea, though we have known Christ after the flesh, yet now henceforth know we him no more. Therefore if any man be in Christ, he is a new creature: old things are passed away; behold, all things are become new.*

Remember, the eclipse is over. The only way you'll have new life in your relationship is to stay in the Son.

Let's conclude with a final revelation from this story. Notice the Bible doesn't give all the details about why this man was paralyzed. In other words, if God thought it was that important, the story would have been different. They would have been lowering him to Jesus saying, "This man was trampled by a camel..." or "He fell into a ditch..." This lack of details revealed to my spirit that God didn't emphasize what went wrong because there are things in our lives He chooses to keep under cover.

If you're paralyzed, God's not interested in airing your dirty laundry. He simply wants you to seek after Him with a heart that says, "Lord, I know You can help me to walk again." And when you do, He'll give you power to rise up from the past carrying the thing that used to carry you. Your pain will purify you for the future and release the power of God in your relationship. Are you ready for the next level?

Endnotes

1. Sol Steinmetz, et al. *Webster's American Family Dictionary* (New York, New York: Random House, Inc., 1998), 687.

2. Ibid., 314.

CHAPTER 3

THE TRUTH ABOUT
MEN AND WOMEN

*...If ye continue in my word, then are ye my disciples indeed;
and ye shall know the truth, and the truth shall make you free.*
John 8:31–32

Honesty is a spiritual magnet for godly relationships. That's why Satan tries to weave his deception by shading the truth about who we really are. The world knows men and women are from different planets, so why do we avoid dealing with the real issues in the church? Hear me. Believers need to get honest; we need to go beyond surface issues because there are more marital problems in the body of Christ than on the street. That's sad.

It's getting to the point that singles don't want to get married and couples don't want to stay married...*which brings us back to the need for a washing.* We need to let God's Word and prophetic insight bring understanding of who we are, how we're built, and how God wants us to interact as men and women. Why? Because even if you love God, you can miss the mark in your marriage. How can you learn to love someone when you have no wisdom about who he or she is (or who you really are, for that matter) in the spirit realm?

So let's start fresh by getting a basic, Holy Ghost understanding of the sexes. Then we'll move on in the following chapters with the day-to-day issues of learning to become a real husband or wife and building your family's future.

My years of pastoral experience have taught me two basic truths. *Men have issues, and women have personalities.*

So, sister, it doesn't matter where your man came from. If he's human, he has issues. And like my wife says, you don't marry perfection. You marry potential. So think of it this way: His issues are what saved him for you. They kept him from marrying somebody else and allowed him to be there for your divine appointment. The question is, do you have the power to release his potential in God?

On the other hand, brother, a woman's personality will reflect your issues. One of my in-laws told me, "You're really special...because Juanita has a few personalities." I laughed and responded, "Yeah, she sure does; about forty-two-and-a-half of them. That's not bad, though, because I have seventy-three." A man has to make sure he has as many personalities as his partner so that when she shifts, he can shift. If you have only two personalities and your wife has forty, you're in big trouble. That means thirty-eight times out of forty, you're going to be lost.

A man I respect once told me, "Son, a woman's different every day." This saved me from a whole lot of trouble, since at the time I expected a woman to be consistent like I was...and she's not created to be that way. Let me explain. God created Adam to till the ground, so he functioned best with specific things to do in an environment that seldom changed. Then He fashioned Eve to establish the home, so she was best suited to multi-task in a constantly changing environment.

The bottom line is the Bible teaches both men and women are builders in God's kingdom. The Hebrew root word for both "son" (Strong's, #H1121) and "daughter" (Strong's, #H1323) is *banah*, which means, "to build" (Strong's, #H1129). Therefore, the roles of men and women are equally important. We simply build in different ways.

Here's the revelation. If you can approach your relationship by understanding that he's going to perceive and handle things one way, or she's going to understand and deal with things another...*together*, you'll cover all of the bases. *Together*, one person taking care of one aspect and the other functioning in another, you can have a good reward for your efforts. You can help each other to succeed in all that you do. Ecclesiastes 4:7–12 says,

> *Then I returned, and I saw vanity under the sun. There is one alone, and there is not a second; yea, he hath neither child nor brother: yet is there no end of all his labour; neither is his eye satisfied with riches; neither saith he, For whom do I labour, and bereave my soul of good? This is also vanity, yea, it is a sore travail. Two are better than one; because they have a good reward for their labour. For if they fall, the one will lift up his fellow: but woe to him that is alone when he falleth; for he hath not another to help him up. Again, if two lie together, then they have heat: but how can one be warm alone? And if one prevail*

against him, two shall withstand him; and a threefold cord is not quickly broken.

If God isn't a vital part of your marriage, it can easily fail. But if He's in "the midst," nothing can tear it down. So in all of your getting, get wisdom about how He wants you to build your relationship.

The Dual Responsibility of a Man

Let's take a look at the two most important responsibilities I believe a man must fulfill in his marriage. They both deal with understanding and communication, which is a paradox, since women tend to perceive and communicate more readily than men. God often has to deal with us to take the lead in two key areas...*dwelling with knowledge of her needs and telling her what we need.*

First Peter 3:7 says,

Likewise, ye husbands, dwell with them according to knowledge, giving honour unto the wife, as unto the weaker vessel, and as being heirs together of the grace of life; that your prayers be not hindered.

If you don't learn everything your wife is—her personality, seasons, days, times, attitudes, and dispositions—you won't be able to dwell with her according to knowledge.

Let me break it down. You have to learn from dwelling with her when you've waited too long to give her flowers or what she liked (or didn't like) the last time you took her out. For example, maybe you took her to a fast food restaurant, and she wanted more time and atmosphere. She wanted a deeper experience, something with more "personality." She didn't want to be rushed through a meal.

A woman wants you to know what she needs. It's like she's always saying, "Feel how I'm feeling." And she doesn't want to explain! She wants to know, "Can you feel me? Can you feel that I'm starving for you to say what I need?"

Let's say you have young children. She could be feeling, "I'm starving for you to be able to realize that I need two days away from the children, and I need you to find a baby-sitter. I need you to surprise me. I need you to pack my bags, put me in a car, and take me away for a weekend. It's been three years since I've had a break, and I don't ask you for much. *Can you feel me*...or do I have to walk around with an attitude for four months in order for you to get the picture that I'm burned out?"

If you know that she responds a certain way when you do something that she loves, and you haven't done it for five months, don't act stupid! When she starts handing you frozen dinners and pop-up waffles, don't be surprised. You have to sacrifice and become a detective. Know why she likes a certain brand of shoes, perfume, or lotion...or why she likes to go to certain places.

Here's another example. All women have a favorite male actor. They'll only tell men who it is, though, when they know our attitudes can handle it. In this situation, the best thing you can do is take her to see one of his movies. She'll love you afterwards! Hypothetically, suppose her favorite actor is Denzel Washington. When a new movie of his comes out and she says, "I'm going to go see it with my girlfriends," she probably means, "You can't handle being with me, so I'm going to go see it with my girlfriends while you watch the football game."

What she really wants to say is, "I wish you would take me. I love you more than I love Denzel; I just like the fact that he's a great actor, and he looks good..." As a man, this can bruise your ego. So you react and say, "Well, you go ahead with your girlfriends. I'm going to hang with the guys." What you should do is respond by saying, "You know what? Let me take you. He's a sharp-looking man." As the man, you have the first responsibility because God expects you to love her *according to knowledge.*

Now let's go to Proverbs 18:22 for a man's second divine challenge.

> *Whoso findeth a wife findeth a good thing, and obtaineth favour of the LORD.*

Why is this a challenge? *Although there are many women, only one can be your wife.* I believe this scripture identifies the man's role to release the "wife" that lives inside of a woman. How are you supposed to do this? That's right...by telling her what you need. If you're single, this means you have to start by being honest with her about who you are—because when you get married, you'll need to be open with her on a much deeper level.

Let me clarify. I'm not talking about telling a woman you need three meals a day, clean clothes, and things like that; that's not what makes her your wife. A maid can do these things. A hired servant can wash clothes. You can hire somebody to clean the house. A woman doesn't have to clean the house to be your wife! She doesn't have to vacuum the floors or wash dishes to be your helpmeet. *A woman only becomes your wife when she can meet your deepest needs.*

Let's say I hired a woman to clean the house. She could be very attractive, but she can't be my wife. A wife is a person I can look in the eyes and say, "I need you to pray for me because I'm dealing with some issues from my childhood. I've got a bad temper, so whenever you see me about to lose it, I need you to put your hand on my shoulder and tell me, 'Honey, I understand who you are…and this isn't going to hold you back.' " I tell my wife what really matters.

A woman may think a man needs her body, but that isn't true. A man really needs love, and God knows this; that's what He fashioned a wife to do. When a woman loves, she gives a lot more than her body. She loves by giving herself. The problem is, many men try to embrace only her physical sensuality. For this reason, a lot of husbands don't truly have a wife. They haven't learned how to share with her from the depths of their spirit. If the only reason you got married was to have sexual intimacy, then you don't have a wife. You have a partner in sex…and you need to change.

A man has to be honest with his wife about his issues. For example, he could share something like, "If you see me struggling, it's because my father died when I was young and there are some things I wasn't taught. I may not be the husband I need to be right now, but I'm trying to find a male mentor who can speak into my life. In fact, you may see my temper flare up, but I'm never going to hit you or hurt you. I just need you to let me get it out. Let me walk out of the house and *deal with me*, and then I'll come back—but please don't reject me because I have issues."

When a man learns to share with his wife this way, she holds the ability to heal him. Oh yes, *he who finds a wife definitely finds a good thing!* He who finds a person who can heal his wounds finds a good thing. A wife will come to you and say, "You know what, baby? I found these videos that deal with childhood areas, and I want to watch them with you so that I can know more about you. In fact, I watched one of them for a little while, and I got to know you so much better. Let's see if these can help." *She'll start trying to find help for you because she's your helpmeet.*

If I don't tell my wife who I am, she can never help me to become greater than I was. When I share my needs with her, she helps me. She loves me that way. A woman will never reject a man who loves her enough to tell her the truth.

The True Nature of a Woman

Let's go back to Adam and Eve. God commanded Adam to till the ground, which rarely changes. Seasons change, so the ground may change a little from time to time, but basically, dirt is dirt. On the other hand, the woman's job is to bruise the head of Satan...and he's always moving, stalking, and seeking whom he may devour (Genesis 2, 3; 1 Peter 5:8). The enemy's thoughts are always moving around from place to place. And it's the woman's job to use her heel to bruise his demonic head.

Juanita confirmed this when she was teaching on the "Proverbs 31 Woman." The eighteenth verse of Proverbs 31 reads,

> *...her lamp goes not out, but it burns on continually through the night [of trouble, privation, or sorrow, warning away fear, doubt, and distrust]* (AMP).

Juanita read this verse and declared, "I always seek to keep my spiritual Light on, because my job is to ward off fear and distrust, and to cancel the spirit of doubt in my house." I'm blessed by the spiritual sensitivity of my wife. She stays in step with what God has anointed her to do as a strong, virtuous woman.

So, brother, if you try to keep your wife "consistent," then some things that are supposed to be *bruised*, *destroyed*, and *removed* will never be purged from your relationship. Don't try to make her consistent (in a manly way), for her job is to fight and ward off the enemy so he never gets a foothold in your home.

While you're tilling the ground, she's preparing the spirit of the place where you rest. You're both hitting all of the bases, and God will bless your labors of love. However, if she's trying to please you and do *your* job, then she can't be herself...and she'll be miserable. If a woman doesn't fulfill her responsibility in the spirit realm, she'll be upset around you all the time. She'll put you up on the roof until she gets enough air to breathe. Guaranteed.

The paradox is you'll be arguing with your wife when in reality you're arguing with yourself—because you tried to make her *you*. And when you can't get what you want out of her, *you get an attitude.* Listen to wisdom. Let her anointing flow so that she can bless you and establish a strong spiritual atmosphere in your home. It's foolish to try to make your wife become something she's not.

A woman discerns from a place that a man cannot begin to comprehend. She's able to tap into a realm where a man has no real sensory discernment of a matter, and there's a reason for this. God fashioned Eve by putting Adam into a deep sleep and then taking her out of his side (Genesis 2:21–22).

The revelation is that Adam had never been to sleep before this experience. This is the first time the Bible recorded he slept. God had to put Adam to sleep because He'd given him 24-hour dominion over the earth.

In other words, Adam didn't need to rest. He was operating on a heavenly standard. His body didn't get tired, and it wasn't going to die. It was already in the eternal realm of existence: perfect health, perfect strength, and perfect rest. When Adam sinned, he detonated a bomb inside of his physical body that we call death, so his body began to disintegrate. Therefore, it needed to have rest to regenerate what had already started disintegrating. *Are you still with me?*

When God put Adam to sleep, it was the first time man had to deal with his subconscious. He wasn't awake, so everything God was doing had to be stored subconsciously. Spiritually, Eve came out of the deepest part of his being. She was fashioned *from him* when he was unconscious, and then she was presented *to him* after he woke up. No wonder women can be such a mystery!

I believe this is also why a woman never seems to get tired. A man can work from 9:00 a.m. to 5:00 p.m., and then come home completely burned out. On the other hand, a woman can be up at 5:00 a.m., still be going strong at 5:00 p.m., and keep going until midnight—without taking a break. And she still has more energy than he does! A woman can endure much more discomfort for a much longer period of time than her male counterpart. She definitely doesn't operate from the same realm.

In fact, from what I've seen, more women run long distance marathons than men. They have extended energy. A woman's only problem with endurance is her strength. A man is technically stronger, but he has less endurance. A woman isn't as strong as a man, but she has more endurance. Another paradox.

And let's not even talk about a woman in the kitchen. In general, it's hilarious to put a man in the kitchen. Many of us have major problems just trying to make one item of the meal work. Put a woman in the kitchen, though, and she can make seven different things happen at the same time…and there's no confusion in the midst of it.

The Challenges of a Real Woman

I need to say something about submission here because it's a major challenge that God presents to a wife. (I go into more detail in the upcoming chapters.) As a woman, you possess incredible, godly attributes. You can perceive, discern, and diversify with seemingly no effort at all. You can literally work around the clock juggling the needs of others along with your own. So when you think about what happened after Eve was enticed to enjoy the fruit of something (something that was never meant for her), it probably irks you.

Let me help you. God knew what was going to happen before Eve was enticed. He allowed the sin to surface as part of the bigger plan. Sound familiar? So if you embrace God's wisdom as we move through this book, He'll honor you. God will bless you with even deeper realms of glory as well as rich fruit in your marriage and family.

If you're single, you have another divine challenge. Although God expects a man to "find" his wife, He expects you to draw him by *being real*. You see, there isn't a shortage of men. There's a shortage of true women who are waiting for a true man—because when a man *finds* a real woman, he won't let her go. On the other hand, when he knows he can be flaky, then he'll settle into that routine. Matthew 13:44 says,

> *Again, the kingdom of heaven is like unto treasure hid in a field; the which when a man hath found, he hideth, and for joy thereof goeth and selleth all that he hath, and buyeth that field.*

When a man finds a real woman in you, when he knows that he's found a "good thing," he'll buy you everything you want to make sure you stay in his life. He'll take you around the neighborhood saying, "Baby, what kind of car do you want? What kind of house do you want? No, you don't have to worry." When you get real and give a man something he's never found before (and it's not between the sheets!), you're going to get married. When he finds a heart that understands him, it won't be long.

He'll marry you as quickly as he can, for the truth of the matter is, he'll see the lines forming…"Uh, oh. Here comes John. There goes Jerry. I'd better do this really quick." And to be honest, the harder it is for him to get your attention, the better it will be for his ego. (Keep it real, though! Don't play games with God.) A man is built to work hard and consistently in order to find and release something of great value. And once he finds you, he'll protect you…like priceless treasure. He'll literally go crazy if somebody doesn't treat you right.

When you're a real woman, a real man will show up. However, if you're timid, you'll settle for less than God's best. Don't be paralyzed by the sin of neediness. Don't let the need to feel needed keep you from possessing the promises of God. Let me explain. Your neediness will draw a needy man. And he won't have anything to meet your needs because he's selfish. He'll try to control your personality and keep you from developing to your fullest potential.

One more thing. *Don't let the word **boyfriend** stumble out of your mouth.* Why? When you call for a boy, that's what you're likely to get: a selfish, immature child. Then when he doesn't graduate or mature in your relationship, you'll be disappointed. The truth of the matter is that you've already dictated a destiny in his spirit *with your words.*

It's simple. *A real man isn't hard to find when the beacon within you is real.* From the time I first met her, Juanita shone with the glory of God. She captivated me. It didn't take long before I knew she would be my wife. Take her advice, virtuous woman. Let your garments exemplify righteousness. It draws people to the temple of God within you. And it will make a man look at you and say, "I want you to be mine!"

Let me tell you when you're really ready to get married: when you can say without reservation, "This is my lord." *Ouch!* I can just hear you saying, "I'm not looking for a lord in my life; my Lord's up in heaven." This is the problem. You don't have a man because you're not willing to treat him the same way you would treat Jesus. First Peter 3:1–6 says,

> *Likewise, ye wives, be in subjection to your own husbands; that, if any obey not the word, they also may without the word be won by the conversation of the wives; while they behold your chaste conversation coupled with fear....For after this manner in the old time the holy women also, who trusted in God,*

adorned themselves, being in subjection unto their own husbands: even as Sara obeyed Abraham, calling him lord: whose daughters ye are, as long as ye do well, and are not afraid with any amazement.

When a woman can find the lord in a man and a man can find the *wife* in a woman, that's the beginning of a true, godly romance.

It All Comes Back to Truth

Too many people are struggling in their relationships because they haven't developed the capacity to be honest with themselves about who they really are. So whether you're single or married, now is the time to start dealing with the *real you*. Let the wisdom of God wash your life so that you can have a powerful, intimate marriage.

If you're single, don't think you're supposed to marry every man or woman who happens to minister to your spirit. And, sister, stop believing every man who walks into the church is your husband! In fact, don't believe it until God tells him *and* you. When you become enticed for a man and start believing he's the one God sent to you, it won't be long before you start acting like it. Then you'll start becoming soulish with him—getting to know him out of the desire to be his wife. If you're not careful, you'll end up becoming his wife outside of the counsel of God's Word.

And, brother, it's the same for you. Don't jump to conclusions out of enticement and think, "Ooh, I believe she's my wife." Before too long, you'll start trying to be her husband long before you ever get married. *This is dangerous*, for you have no idea the kind of responsibility God's getting ready to put on you for that woman.

Do things God's way. And remember…a woman just wants to know that her husband loves her more than anybody else. And a man needs to know that his wife will hear who he is and help him to become better.

Are You Ready to Change?

Are you ready for a new level in your marriage? Do you sense God is challenging you to change in your relationship? Then get real…be brutally honest, for it's easy to shout and rejoice when you're believing God to do something *for you.* It's much harder to let God do something *in you.* Let Him purge, wash, and make you clean—because you don't want to love God and still miss the mark in your marriage. Learn how to love the way He's made you to love…and it will keep getting better.

II

The Beginning of "Us"

God's Wisdom for Establishing Your Marriage

> I used to think no man could find a virtuous woman...but that was before a godly man found me. Now I understand God's true process for becoming one.
> –JBW

- Embracing her emotions and releasing her dreams
- Multiplying his vision and meeting his needs
- Making love that lasts forever

The heart of her husband trusts in her confidently...She comforts, encourages, and does him only good as long as there is life within her.
Proverbs 31:11–12 AMP

CHAPTER 4

HELP, LORD, I NEED
A GODLY HUSBAND

**Husbands, love your wives [be affectionate and sympathetic with them]
and do not be harsh or bitter or resentful toward them.
Colossians 3:19 AMP**

My wife has been through many disappointments with
men. On two different occasions she was abandoned by a fiancé who immediately turned around and married another
woman. There were other times she suffered emotional and
physical abuse and was used to satisfy a man's personal and fi-
nancial needs. That's why I cherish her and love God so
much—because she emerged from it all a true Proverbs 31
woman. She's the kind of wife that makes me want to become
the man of her dreams.

While we were making plans to get married, she initially
wanted a ten-carat diamond ring. So we flew to Chicago and
went to Tiffany's with some friends. After a round of professional advice and measurements, Juanita and I found a very
special seven-carat setting. It was perfect. Everybody in the

room said, "That's it!" Then I looked at the price tag and thought, *House.*

It didn't matter. I was glad to count the cost. After all, she wasn't just going to be my woman anymore…she was becoming my wife.

By the time we finished shopping, we'd bought two seven-carat engagement rings, along with the seven-carat wedding band. All in all, that's twenty-one carats of diamonds and sapphires. I have news for you—*I'll never leave her!*

Seriously, though, the purchases challenged me, but I realized the significance of my investments. Twenty-one carats don't hold a candle to the value of my wife. The price tag pales when I think of what she means to me and to our destiny in God.

The fact is, before we walked down the aisle and said, "I do," we each wore a temporary ring that *together* cost about $53.00. And we're always going to cherish them because they demonstrate our commitment to "little things." *When you get married, it's not about having it all.* Marriage is about working toward each other's dreams and desires, starting from wherever you may be *right now.*

I have learned the most important thing I can do as a husband is to truly love and care for my wife. It's not fair to marry a woman and not be concerned with fulfilling her dreams. After all, Ephesians 5:25–30 confirms this is what being a godly husband is all about.

> *Husbands, love your wives, even as Christ also loved the church, and gave himself for it; that he might sanctify and cleanse it with the washing of water by the word, that he might present it to himself a glorious church, not having spot, or wrinkle, or any such*

thing; but that it should be holy and without blemish. So ought men to love their wives as their own bodies. He that loveth his wife loveth himself. For no man ever yet hated his own flesh; but nourisheth and cherisheth it, even as the Lord the church: for we are members of his body, of his flesh, and of his bones.

From my experience, men generally understand what God is saying in this passage, but we tend to skip over the details. We miss the process. So I want to break it down in a practical way in order to help us better understand how to walk out this revelation from a renewed understanding in our spirits.

Bear with me, because we're going to deal with some areas that will definitely challenge your flesh. Understand, though, my goal is to bring a balanced perspective to what many are currently teaching in the church. Too often we give people a passion for getting married without tapping their desire to understand their purpose in a relationship. We must balance passion and purpose. And, brother, when we do, the true status and value of women will be restored, for all too often they've been beaten up by male chauvinistic doctrines.

A Godly Man Is Drawn to Love

Let's start by reading Colossians 3:18–19 from the Amplified Bible.

Wives, be subject to your husbands [subordinate and adapt yourselves to them], as is right and fitting and your proper duty in the Lord. Husbands, love your wives [be affectionate and sympathetic with them] and do not be harsh or bitter or resentful toward them.

I'd like to approach this passage by using a process I call *reverse hermeneutics.* In other words, I'm going to start at the end and work my way back to the beginning. In verse 19, husbands are clearly commanded to love their wives, but wives aren't given this same command. There's a reason for that.

A woman loves automatically. She's made to love, so she can't just flip a switch and turn off her feelings. I believe this is why many women stay in abusive relationships. They love the man so deeply that it seems impossible to leave him. Compassion keeps drawing them back. So these women stay in a relationship they really hate because they love so much to love.

Loving isn't a problem for a wife; it's a problem for the husband. Hear me: Men aren't built to love; they're drawn to it. A man doesn't love automatically. He can learn how to love, but it's definitely not automatic. The secret about a man's love is once he's found a "good thing," it draws him into loving a woman completely. The question is, will he be able to love the parts of his wife that he hasn't seen yet?

A Godly Man Must Embrace Weakness

A man must learn to love his wife by developing the capacity to embrace her weaknesses. So, sister, you may want a man to love you for what you present to him as strengths, but you really need a man who can love your weaknesses. The truth of the matter is, if a man can love your weaknesses, *he'll adore your strengths.*

Most women want a man to love their strengths and tolerate their weaknesses. This presents a challenge because when a man merely tolerates a woman's weaknesses, it's hard for her to fully submit to him...because she knows he doesn't love her completely. Hear me, sister. If you have a man who truly loves your weaknesses, you'll gladly submit to him...*because you feel protected.* A wife will always struggle against her husband when she feels he can't protect her vulnerabilities. He continually picks at what she's doing wrong instead of celebrating how she's trying to get it right.

A godly man will learn to be sensitive to this dilemma. He'll sense when you're crying out, "I'm still dealing with my pain. And if you can love me like this, I can submit everything I am to you. And I'll love whatever you need me to love in you because I know you can't love automatically. I'll submit myself to love you, for as you love my weaknesses, I'll be able to love who you're in the process of becoming."

Yes, a godly man will embrace the fact that you'll never be perfect, but he'll learn to desire you in the midst of your weaknesses. And understand this: Though a woman never wants to fall short in any area, you can't always realize this desire. When the inevitable happens, a godly man won't abandon you. He'll appreciate that you tried and help you get back to where you want to be.

A Godly Man Must Cover a Woman's Emotions

Colossians 3:19 tells us a husband must *be affectionate.* In other words, brother, the way you secure your wife is to make sure you bring attention to every emotional, social, and sensual need. You must give her affection when and how *she needs it.* As a godly man, part of loving your wife is understanding her emotional need—because women are highly emotional.

So, sister, if a man doesn't understand your emotions, he'll never be able to love you. Your emotions ignite your "personalities." They cause you to change...day by day and moment by moment. Knowing this, a godly man will learn to wake up each morning and immediately find out where you're at, since he wants to learn how to love you that day. Believe me, this is the wisdom of God.

When your husband realizes you are *consistently emotional*, he'll learn to find the temperature of your emotions—because your emotional patterns are always changing according to how he relates to you. This puts a lot of responsibility on your husband because he'll miss the mark until he can take time to study you in all of your environments.

So you must learn how to invite him into every emotional environment. That way he'll be able to learn who you are. Your husband must understand when you're calm, or under stress. He must be able to discern when you don't want to cook, don't feel like being a wife, or don't want to work on a job. In short, he must learn your emotional temperature, for in order to show you affection, he has to understand where to focus his attention.

He has to learn your psychological path because a woman's psyche is intimately connected to her spirit. If a man can learn how to understand your thought patterns and deal with your dreams, he'll be able to discern what's in your spirit.

So, brother, don't assume anything in your marriage. Get in the habit of asking how your wife is feeling. For example, when trouble is in the air (instead of assuming it's that time of the month for her), try asking, "Baby, did I make you mad last night?" Don't just assume she and her girlfriend didn't have a good conversation that day. Cover her. Take action, for if your perception of her emotional temperature is wrong, she'll feel uncovered and you'll really have a situation.

Remember, a woman wants you to feel her struggle and ask what's wrong, *so that you can answer it.* There are times she won't say anything just to see if you can be sensitive to her needs. Actually, I also believe this ties back into her problem with introducing her emotions—*because they're like hidden treasure.* You must identify and draw them out. So once she draws you in to loving her completely, you can *draw her out* into trusting your ability to cover her.

Walk to her emotions—anticipate them—by demonstrating you care. Notice I didn't say show *affection*; that comes afterwards. In order to demonstrate care, you must ask, "How are you? Do you need anything? Is it time for you to get a break? Do you need to go shopping?" Identify the need by showing you care, and then focus on giving her affection.

This is especially true if a woman was never able to develop a meaningful relationship with her father or with other males in her immediate family. Maybe every time she tried to reach out, she was shut off because her dad had other priorities. He either had to go to work, or was hungry, or maybe wanted to catch a football game. As a result, she didn't gain a balanced perspective in relating to the opposite sex.

Every woman has experienced various levels of drama in her childhood. She might have been tampered with by an uncle; abused by her mother; or hindered by her father. For example, her father may have said, "I'm not paying for your college; I don't have it. I'm not rich like that." And because of that, her emotions have been damaged. So whenever a man says, "I'm not paying for it," unresolved anger triggers in her emotions and she's headed for trouble.

So at times you may have to become more than a husband; you may have to become a pseudo-father—embracing the places her dad never hugged and affirming the things he never acknowledged. (And to be fair, this doesn't mean Dad didn't love her. He may not have had the time or knowledge to speak these things into her life.) So even though she's a woman, there may be certain areas where she's like a child. For example, your wife might be twenty-eight years old, but in a certain part of her emotions, she's really sixteen.

That's why a husband has to identify the emotional level of her need and satisfy it on that level (notice I didn't say sexually!). If you learn to meet your wife's emotional level, you'll gain a deeper inference of covering her. It's like building a tent. You put down stakes, set up pillars, and then cast the covering. You have to be patient, though, because you can only put down stakes when she shares with you about her pain. It takes a lot for a woman to become vulnerable and acknowledge her scars.

Husband, let me say this again. It's *your responsibility* to study your wife and identify her emotional needs.

A woman will always want to know, even after she becomes your wife, if she can trust you with the truth of who she really is. Her spirit cries, "If I tell you the truth about me, will that make you uncover me, or cover me more?" Be careful; if she feels like you're more withdrawn when she shows you more truth, she'll shut down the romance and embrace you only as a friend. Even in marriage! So if something feels awkward in your relationship, brother, check the woman's temperature…and then minister to her need. Demonstrate you care, and healing will come.

The one thing that locked my wife and I together (besides obedience) was our encounter at Starbuck's. I shared a part of me that I couldn't reveal to anybody else, and she did the same. *I treasured this*, for it takes a very mature woman to tell a man who she really is. And when all has been said and done—when the weave, shoulder pads, and surface matters are out of the way—a woman with deep emotions is waiting to be acknowledged. She's hoping you don't drop her in front of her friends, ignore her in front of her family, or embarrass her in front of her co-workers. A woman needs your covering. First Peter 5:6–7 says,

> *Humble yourselves therefore under the mighty hand*
> *of God, that he may exalt you in due time: casting all*
> *your care upon him; for he careth for you.*

This is a mystery because it humbles a woman to trust a man with her emotions. Yet, when she knows you care, she'll literally begin to cast her anxieties upon you—because her spirit knows you've been anointed to minister to her need.

A Godly Man Must Not Be Resentful

According to Colossians 3:19, a godly man must have a sympathetic spirit: *"...[be affectionate and sympathetic with them] and do not be harsh or bitter or resentful toward them"* (AMP). Another word for sympathy is *compassion*.[1] In short, a godly man should be like Christ. This means he'll be able to go through changes with a woman and not be harsh, bitter, or resentful. Sister, this means he won't snap at you or abuse you just because you can become emotional about things you're dealing with.

This is a tall order for a man. And believe me, it's not going to happen overnight. He must develop the capacity. He has to weather the times when you get loud and upset. He has to look past when certain parts of your body begin to communicate anger. You know what I'm saying. When a woman gets angry with a man, her hips begin to speak, her neck gets busy, and her eyebrows and eyes become like daggers. And if that isn't enough, her tongue grows about an inch or two…then she leans forward and puts her finger up in his face.

In all of this shifting, a man has to learn how not to be harsh, bitter, or resentful. He has to have the ability to hold back harshness, pull back bitterness, and make sure he doesn't destroy and annihilate her emotions. And, brother, in all the shifting, it's very important you don't start to resent that you married her. Once a man starts resenting he's in one situation, every other situation starts to look better. I'm not condoning this; I'm simply stating the truth.

So, brother, don't become harsh, bitter, or resentful. It will only make you vulnerable to enticement. When you're resentful, even old, dead relationships start looking better than the one you're committed to now. And sister, don't give your husband something he doesn't deserve. Don't abuse God's command for him to love your weaknesses. This way he won't have any reason to start resenting.

Let me clarify. I'm not saying you shouldn't be honest with your husband; but when your emotions, psyche, or sensuality give him emotions he doesn't deserve, be honest with him afterwards and admit you shouldn't have done it. If you don't explain this to a man, it will be difficult for him to be affectionate and sympathetic. He might not be able to hold back harshness or stop bitterness and resentment. *Remember this: If you keep giving a man something you can't explain, then you'll cause him to resent what he doesn't understand.* Then you'll really have problems.

A godly man will always be in the process of learning how to embrace your weaknesses until he can get you to love *who you're becoming.* Oh, yes! When your man can hold his peace and not become harsh with you, *he understands you.* On the other hand, if he argues and debates with you—and kills your emotions—he doesn't know who you are. He doesn't have the capacity yet to really learn how to love you; he must grow into it. Be encouraged, though. A man who loves God will always embrace the challenge to change...especially when he knows that he's found a "good thing" in you.

A Godly Man Must Release a Woman's Dreams

In the process of becoming a godly husband, it can be hard learning how not to break or bend while answering a woman's dreams, desires, and needs. However, as you embrace the deepest parts of your wife, *she'll awaken to you.* She'll push you to new and better places, and she'll allow you to pursue your dreams. If you'll embrace your wife's desires, there's nothing she won't do for you.

Here's a word of wisdom. Take your wife out to dinner and say, "All right, honey, I have my notepad and pen. Tell me everything you want to do in your lifetime. And then tell me from start to finish what you want to do in the next six months...year...two years....five years." After she shares with you, make a commitment to her that she'll never fail in getting it done.

Never rob a woman of her dreams, for if you do, she'll regret knowing you. When a woman shares her dreams with you, she doesn't want you to shrug your shoulders, throw up your hands, and make excuses. She's expecting you to at least acknowledge her desires. And if you can't do something toward her dreams right away, start by doing something that says *I'm trying*. A woman will always celebrate a man who tries, versus a man who flat-out ignores her.

Now, sister, here's your challenge. Whenever you really want to grow in life, you must learn to tell your husband what you really want. You may have a girlfriend with whom you share a few of your desires, but I've found a woman rarely trusts another woman with all of her dreams—because there are some things you don't want another woman to know about you. If you do, there's something wrong with how you relate to the same sex.

A woman should never be drawn to you the way a man is. If she is, you could fall into the trap of trusting her to cover you (as only a man should). Need I say more? Watch out for the enemy's devices.

A woman tends to be drawn to something that *echoes her*, but if she's drawn to the wrong thing, she struggles with knowing how to say it's not what she needs. And this reveals the secret of a man's greatest ministry to his wife. He holds the ability to hear her desires and echo them back to her. That's the beginning of releasing her dreams.

If a man wants to impress a woman, he only has to *listen* and *do*—because even though a woman is a mystery, she's not hard to please if a man listens and does the little things that she desires.

A Godly Man Will Always Receive Something in Return

Be encouraged, man of God, because a woman will multiply whatever you give her and give it back to you. If you truly love her, she'll multiply it back to you. If you give her a whole lot of pain and frustration, however, she'll multiply that and give it right back. This is where you must learn to turn the corner in your relationship. Stop giving your wife negativity and start giving her understanding. Give her calmness, peace, attention, and support.

My wife was ministering to our congregation recently about how we've both come through a lot of hurts in our past and are continuing to grow in our relationship. During this message, she said something that really impacted me: "Certain things won't be healed. They can't be touched, so you have to become sensitive to the part that hurts. When I don't feel good enough, and I ask my husband, 'Why are you with me?' or 'Why do you love me?'—that's when he takes me into his arms and says, 'Come on, baby, it's going to be all right.' That's the day I get three dozen roses and he jumps on a plane just to spend one hour with me."

I'm not bragging about myself; I'm confirming what a husband can do to bless his wife—because God will turn around and bless you, if you love His daughter the way you should. I remember sometime after buying her rings at Tiffany's (which was like buying a house and a couple of cars!), my wife came out to me and said, "What's your favorite kind of car?" I smiled and said, "One day I want a quad four twin turbo, 800 horsepower beast. I want it no less than 800 horsepower. I want it to go from 0 to 60 miles per hour in three seconds." What can

I say? I want a beast of a car—but I realize it's not going to happen overnight. It will come with time. It's all in the process.

Listen to me. If you don't like what you're getting out of your relationship, then change what you've been giving. Brother, dwell with your wife according to knowledge and love her so deeply that it unlocks the treasure in her heart. And sister, let God begin to renew His purpose for you in marriage. Give your husband the truth of who you really are so that he can echo your dreams.

Endnote

1. Steinmetz, *Webster's Dictionary*, 946–47.

Chapter 5

Help, Lord, I Need a Godly Wife

Wives, be subject to your husbands [subordinate and adapt yourselves to them], as is right and fitting and your proper duty in the Lord.
Colossians 3:18 AMP

A woman who is covered by a godly husband is a powerful revelation. And no, it doesn't mean she's incapable of doing things on her own. It's actually quite the opposite, according to Proverbs 31:10–12:

> *A capable, intelligent, and virtuous woman—who is he who can find her? She is far more precious than jewels and her value is far above rubies or pearls. The heart of her husband trusts in her confidently and relies on and believes in her securely, so that he has no lack of [honest] gain or need or dishonest spoil. She comforts, encourages, and does him only good as long as there is life within her* (AMP).

Juanita is a spiritual powerhouse, yet she consistently humbles herself to become my helpmeet. On one occasion, while she was speaking at a series of revival meetings, I arrived after her to discover she'd already made arrangements for us to have an entire day alone. Sensing my need and desire for us to be together, she didn't attend the meeting that evening, and we had a blessed time. *That's a virtuous woman.* I count it a privilege to be her covering.

I think the problem arises in many marriages when a wife is uncovered. She comes under subjection to a man who has no relationship with God, so he doesn't have any covering to *cover her!* Therefore, he can't *confidently* trust in her because he hasn't been trustworthy before God on her behalf. The relationship is eclipsed. A godly marriage must have the life of God flowing into it, or growth will be stagnated. And it will be more difficult for the wife to comfort, encourage, and do good things for her husband.

A Virtuous Woman Multiplies Godly Seed

Remember, a woman is created to multiply. So by virtue of God's anointing upon her life, she increases everything she touches. That's why I say, husband, to be careful what you put into your marriage—because it's going to be multiplied and given right back to you. Let's look at how this mystery unfolds in Genesis 1.

> *In the beginning God created the heaven and the earth. And the earth was without form, and void; and darkness was upon the face of the deep. And the Spirit of God moved upon the face of the waters* (Genesis 1:1–2).

When God began the process of creation, the earth was desolate, worthless, and empty (Strong's, #H8414, #H922). Darkness covered a swirling, surging mass of water (Strong's, #H2822/#H2821 and #H8415/#H1949). *And then the Holy*

Spirit moved upon it, which means to "brood...to be relaxed" (Strong's, #H7363). *This is powerful*—because at that very moment, the waters changed. They became pregnant with the presence of God (Strong's, #H4325).

Let me take this one step further. When the Spirit *brooded* upon the waters, He was covering the seeds from heaven. Think about it. An animal broods over its young by sitting on top of the eggs to protect and keep them warm until they hatch. Then the birthing takes place. Let's continue in Genesis 1, verses 9–13:

> *And God said, Let the waters under the heaven be gathered together unto one place, and let the dry land appear: and it was so. And God called the dry land Earth; and the gathering together of the waters called he Seas: and God saw that it was good. And God said, Let the earth bring forth grass, the herb yielding seed, and the fruit tree yielding fruit after his kind, whose seed is in itself, upon the earth: and it was so. And the earth brought forth grass, and herb yielding seed after his kind, and the tree yielding fruit, whose seed was in itself, after his kind: and God saw that it was good. And the evening and the morning were the third day.*

Here's the revelation. The earth was under water until the third day; thus, it was formed while submerged in the transformed waters of the Holy Spirit. When God commanded the waters to be gathered together for dry land to appear...*a birthing took place.* Afterwards, grass, herbs, and trees started springing up from the ground. Stay with me. When a woman is pregnant, the embryo is submerged in her womb until she gives birth. After the baby is born, she cares for the child until it reaches maturity. She multiplies the seed from her womb.

Now let's look at the covering. Before being transformed, the waters were surging and agitated—much like what can happen in a woman's emotions. Yet, when the Spirit of God "relaxed" on the waters, they became pregnant with His presence and were able to form and birth out His seed. So when a husband covers his wife's emotions, she'll multiply his godly seed and return it to him as a blessing.

Remember 1 Peter 5:7 from the last chapter: *"Casting all your care upon him; for he careth for you."* The word *care* comes from a Greek root that means, "to part...disunite" (Strong's, #G3308/#G3307/#G3313). The revelation is this: When a husband covers his wife's emotions, Genesis 1:9 can happen for her in the spirit realm. *"And God said, Let the waters under the heaven be gathered together unto one place, and let the dry land appear...."* In other words, the covering transforms her emotions and helps her give birth to the ministry of a godly wife.

Then God can harness her emotions and use her to bruise the head of the enemy in her household. And everything in her care will "spring up" to maturity. Oh, yes! When a godly wife puts her hands to a thing, it multiplies.

A Virtuous Woman Understands Submission

One day Juanita said to me, "I want you to know that I believe in you. I believe in where you're going because you know where you're going—*but I must believe, and I must follow.*" This struck me. It was so powerful, especially since she made a point to share this at the beginning of our marriage. And, of course, she was echoing something that was already deep in my spirit. *God confirmed that we're truly one flesh.* A man must always lead "knowing," and a woman must always follow "believing."

With this in mind, let's go back to Colossians 3:18 as it reads in the King James Version.

> *Wives, submit yourselves unto your own husbands, as it is fit in the Lord.*

For women, there's some sensitivity connected to the word *submit*, so let's start here. Sister, don't think you're any less important to God because He commands you to *submit* to your husband. Jesus submitted to the Father in order that you, as a virtuous woman, could embrace it. He said, *"I and my Father are one,"* just like husband and wife (John 10:30). He spoke only what the Father told Him, and He did only what the Father revealed for Him to do. Then, when He prayed in Gethsemane before being crucified, take a look at what He did:

> *And he went a little farther, and fell on his face, and prayed, saying, O my Father, if it be possible, let this cup pass from me: nevertheless not as I will, but as thou wilt* (Matthew 26:39).

There is power in submission, for Jesus said unless a seed would fall to the ground and die, it would remain alone. If it dies, it becomes fruitful (John 12:24). So, sister, let me ask you: *Do you believe Jesus was fruitful for God?* Do you want to be like Jesus? Then you must submit—because if you really want to multiply what God has entrusted to your care, submission is the only way to do it.

Now let me say this. I realize the church tends to view submission from one limited perspective. And sometimes it almost comes across like women are dogs that need to sit and be still, not responding to who they really are. This is wrong. Brother, your wife doesn't have to be seen and not heard to be submissive. Think about when Jesus approached the Samaritan woman at the well. Do you think He would have identified and released ministry in her if she wasn't equipped to discern and respond to His voice? (John 4:5–43) Let me bring out some points in this story.

> *There cometh a woman of Samaria to draw water: Jesus saith unto her, Give me to drink. (For his disciples were gone away unto the city to buy meat.) Then saith the woman of Samaria unto him, How is it that thou, being a Jew, askest drink of me, which am a woman of Samaria? for the Jews have no dealings with the Samaritans. Jesus answered and said unto her, If thou knewest the gift of God, and who it is that saith to thee, Give me to drink; thou wouldest have asked of him, and he would have given thee living water. The woman saith unto him, Sir, thou hast nothing to draw with, and the well is deep: from whence then hast thou that living water? Art thou greater than our father Jacob, which gave us the well, and drank thereof himself, and his children, and his cattle? Jesus answered and said unto her, Whosoever drinketh of this water shall thirst again: but whosoever drinketh of the water that I shall give him shall never thirst; but the water that I shall give him shall be in him a well of water springing up into everlasting*

life. The woman saith unto him, Sir, give me this
water, that I thirst not, neither come hither to draw....
The woman then left her waterpot, and went her way
into the city, and saith to the men, Come, see a man,
which told me all things that ever I did: is not this the
Christ? Then they went out of the city, and came unto
him (John 4:7–15, 28–30).

It's interesting that Jesus approached this woman at a deep
well, drew out her true feelings, and then echoed them back to
her. Even more so, He offered her *living water*...pregnant with
the purpose of God. By verse 39, something powerful had already been set into motion:

And many of the Samaritans of that city believed on
him for the saying of the woman, which testified, He
told me all that ever I did.

Can you see that this woman multiplied what Jesus gave
to her, and then returned it to Him? What's more, she didn't
have a husband—since she'd been married five times and was
living with a sixth man—*so Jesus covered her* (John 4:16–18).
Can I suggest to you that this woman saw God in Him that day?
And since He covered her emotionally, she was able to boldly
go back into the city at His command (regardless of her past
mistakes) and reap fruit for the kingdom.

So, brother, if you want a godly wife, start by recognizing
she has the ability *to see God in you.* This means you must
demonstrate the capacity to present God to her—because a
woman isn't fooled when you simply talk about God. She discerns from a much deeper place. It doesn't matter how many
black suits and ties you put on, a woman can tell if there's an

ounce of God in you. She can't be fooled by a man who merely quotes a few scriptures and comes to church a couple of times; *she can discern what's inside of you.*

When a virtuous woman sees God in her husband, she'll gladly submit. (Bear in mind, this doesn't mean he has to be fully matured in Christ; but there will be aspects of God in him that she can see.) And she'll develop the capacity to recognize and acknowledge him as *lord* (1 Peter 3:6). When a godly woman submits to her husband, she activates the anointing of God in his life.

So, sister, if God isn't operating in your marriage, maybe it's because you're not letting Him operate *in you.* Are you recognizing and appreciating who your husband is in God? My wife once said that the devil tries hard to make a woman focus on what her husband *isn't,* instead of *who he is.* If this is your struggle, try to remember…your husband isn't perfect; he's a project. *Praise him for what he is and prayerfully handle yourself when he falls short*—because as a godly wife, you've been anointed to help bring him to completion.

On the other hand, it's difficult for a woman to submit if her husband doesn't know God. And truth be told, deep down, even an unsaved man knows that he needs God to cover his wife, and it provokes something in him. He recognizes that he has a void because he doesn't have the ability to give her what she really needs and desires. Believe me, this man will be miserable until he gives his life to God…and the woman will have to endure a difficult, spiritual struggle.

Let's look again at 1 Peter 3:1–2:

> *Likewise, ye wives, be in subjection to your own husbands; that, if any obey not the word, they also may*

without the word be won by the conversation of the wives; while they behold your chaste conversation coupled with fear.

Let me clarify something. I don't believe a woman should marry a man who doesn't know God. And if truth be told, sister, your husband reflects your level of devotion. So if you were dating an ungodly man and didn't seek God about your marriage, it speaks to how much God was *in you*. It's a reflection of your emotional temperature at that time. There was something in you that allowed *him* to meet a need God was waiting to supply.

Know this—once you've submitted yourself to a man, he's the sole voice and authority to fulfill your needs.

Now, don't let this paralyze you. Instead, let God break this issue off of your life so that you can grow and develop as a virtuous woman—because the greatest thing you could ever do is touch the Lord in your life. And you'll definitely capture His heart if you learn how to submit. Tell me, if your husband doesn't know God, what could be more powerful than praising God during your night season? Wouldn't it be awesome to look at him and say, "Come to bed, my lord?" Think about it. Ponder it in your heart.

If a woman who had five husbands (and was living with a sixth man) could help win a city, God can use you to draw your husband to Christ! Once a man recognizes that the love you have for him *comes from God*, then he'll see the need to seek Him and start learning how to love you completely.

Here's more food for thought. If you study the percentages of diseases between male and female patients, you would see that a woman is more vulnerable to disease than a man. There's a significantly higher occurrence of diseases in women, whether it's tumors, lumps, fibroids, thyroids…*whatever*. This reveals to me there's some type of imbalance that starts speaking in a woman's body when she hasn't learned to submit. Listen, sister, whether you're single or married, uncovered emotions will start speaking through your vessel.

This isn't an easy revelation, but I believe it's true. If you're operating in the spirit and not submitting in the natural, your body will begin to tell you through issues in your flesh. Things will start growing in you against your womanhood because unresolved hurts are living on the inside. Some of these issues may stem from your childhood, others from young adulthood. Some are possibly from your marriage. This is why it's vital for you to bring your husband into your environment. Show him who you really are, for if you don't learn how to resolve the submission issue, you'll end up carrying it.

Forgive me, sister, but let me identify one of the main things you can do to get victory over this dilemma. Stop calling your best friend saying, "You know, girl, he's not right…" and "I just hate the kind of man that always treats me like this…" *You knew he wasn't right from day one!* Now you're being enticed to embrace a spirit that's calling out everything he's doing wrong and nothing he's doing right. And the devil is using this to take both of you down.

Be encouraged. Rise up and become a Proverbs 31 woman, for your relationship doesn't grow from being right; *it grows out of wrongs becoming…* And as long as abuse isn't a factor, you can dwell with him and love him into the presence of God. Remember this: *A man doesn't struggle to lead; he struggles to love.* So if you embrace your anointing to teach him how to love, your husband will rise up in God and help you to embrace submission. Keep in mind, God has given you a unique anointing to increase godly seed in your marriage. So as you submit, *don't forget His promise*:

> *Her children arise up, and call her blessed; her husband also, and he praiseth her* (Proverbs 31:28).

A Virtuous Woman Recognizes Her Assignment

Now, brother, let me get back to you. If you want a godly wife, you need to demonstrate to her that she's worthy of becoming everything you desire for your calling, purpose, and assignment in life. Hear me, if a woman doesn't meet your assignment, she'll never be your wife. And it's the same on the other hand: If you don't meet her assignment, you can never be her husband. Simply bringing home money and putting food on the table doesn't mean much, unless you're helping your wife to fulfill her God-given destiny.

A virtuous woman knows her anointing as a wife is to learn what God has assigned you to do, and then kill everything in the spirit realm that's fighting against it. She'll bruise the head of Satan on your behalf! I found that out one day at Starbuck's when I intervened for Juanita with a man (who had been drinking) as we walked out of the door. He came back against me with a threat, and she almost lost it. And we weren't married at the time. Now that she's my wife, I'm even more confident in her anointing to bruise the enemy's head in prayer.

So, sister, understand your anointing and say to yourself, "I'm not going to let God down in my husband; I'm going to build him up in God. I'm going to speak to him until God becomes so great inside of him that I'll look at him and say,

'My lord, how are you doing today?' " Keep in mind, a virtuous woman is strong enough in God to say these words to him without reservation.

A big part of meeting a man's assignment is understanding his vision. Remember, *a man must lead "knowing," and a woman must follow "believing."* For me, I start by recognizing the most important aspect of my vision is to help Juanita fulfill hers. As a husband, I understand that we have assignments together *and* separately unto the Lord. We are partakers of His grace *together*. So if I misuse my leadership role, my prayers will not be effective (1 Peter 3:7).

Juanita and I have come to the understanding that approximately seventy percent of our vision isn't the same. Thirty percent of what we do matches; this is our common vision. The other seventy percent is comprised of individual assignments. We both make sure to keep each other aware of these assignments and respect them in each other's lives. This way, we can always be ready to help and support when needed.

The point is, we're both on a learning curve. And we're believing that we'll continue to learn in the seventy percent arena while growing in the thirty percent we're able to do together.

My wife has a very powerful ministry—and I'm not asking her to give it up. If I did, I'd be asking her to give up who she is. That would be wrong. I recognize that my wife is called to ministry, but I also know there's much more to her than that. I've studied her; I deal with her *according to knowledge*. Juanita has a very powerful, genius mind—but if I tried to control her, I'd end up losing the benefit of what she contributes to the thirty percent of our commonality. And this middle ground is where we both love to minister together.

As a husband, I can grow in vision as long as we keep what we have in common intact…and then make sure we keep maturing. As we both continue to seek God, He'll take that thirty percent and use it more than either one of our efforts in the seventieth percentile *laboring alone*. So we have common ground and individual assignments—but divine synergy helps keep it all in balance.

Listen to me, brother. Don't fall into the trap of thinking a godly woman can't be as productive in her endeavors as you are in yours. According to Proverbs 31, she's supposed to be! (Make sure both you and your wife listen to Juanita's teaching on the CD that's enclosed with this book—it's by far one of the best, most honest teachings on the subject.) Remember, a virtuous woman won't always look to you to procure what she wants; she comes into a relationship with her own resources, then keeps multiplying them as a godly wife. And if you release her anointing, she'll increase everything she touches in your household. Then you'll have good reason to celebrate her and be highly confident in her abilities.

A Virtuous Woman Wants to Please Her Husband

I appreciate my wife's openness. One day we were together and she asked, "Do I please you?" She continued asking me specific questions until I assured her that I love her just the way she is. She wasn't being emotional; she really wanted to know. I'm confident that if I had said I wanted her to do something differently, she would have immediately started the process to change. My God, how I love my wife!

And brother, when a woman wants to please you, it goes beyond the bedroom. It goes far beyond cooking, washing clothes, and making sure the house is clean. I've already touched on the fact that just because she may cook your breakfast or make the bed, doesn't make her your wife. There are plenty of hired workers who will do these things without having a ring on their finger. The question is, *is your wife meeting your deepest needs?* Is her healing anointing being released in your spirit?

Nowadays, there's a lot of role sharing in relationships. In fact, I believe the word *relationship* communicates that many role responsibilities can be shared (as long as they don't violate the other person's anointing in the home...*we'll go into this later*). So as husband and wife, you must learn each other's roles and define them. Make it work for you. In other words, I might be going to the cleaners this week, and she might be going next week. And if there's a responsibility neither one of us has time for, we can hire somebody to do it.

Before we were married, I knew our lives were going to be so busy that my wife wasn't going to have time to clean the house. And we have so little time together, I didn't want her using it up trying to wash windows! It's better for me to hire somebody to clean and then spend those few hours with my wife. So, husband, it all comes down to *what you believe* your wife's purpose is in your relationship. Certainly, she's more valuable to you than mere creature comforts. Tell me, how is she contributing to your destiny?

Both Juanita and I believe that we'll get out of our relationship what we put into it, spiritually or otherwise. And believe me, she's highly virtuous; she pleases me in every way.

And she's constantly trying to anticipate what I need so that she can make it happen.

For another woman, pleasing your husband may mean you simply show up at his baseball game and root for him as loudly as you can. In fact, be the loudest cheerleader at the game. Even if you don't like baseball, *act like you do*. Pack him a good lunch, put in some vitamins, and carry his Gatorade.

Sit on the front bleacher and record every minute on videotape. Say, "Baby, you're doing good," even though he struck out four times. Comfort him, massage his back; do all of that good stuff. When the game is over, he's going to love you even more—because he understands that baseball may not be your forte, but because you love him, you were willing to invest in what makes him happy. Love him until he learns how godly he is as a husband, and then God will use him to bless your life.

And brother, remember that a godly wife is *yours*, but a woman belongs to everybody else. God expects you to love her completely and bring out the wife He's planted deep in her spirit. Celebrate her when she's virtuous and cover her when she's not. A godly wife will multiply *the seeds you plant* into her life, and she'll give birth to your destiny in God. If you release her anointing, she'll identify and release the God in you.

CHAPTER 6

HELP, LORD, I
WANT GODLY PASSION

*Let marriage be held in honor (esteemed worthy, precious,
of great price, and especially dear) in all things. And thus
let the marriage bed be undefiled (kept undishonored);
for God will judge and punish the unchaste [all guilty of
sexual vice] and adulterous.*
Hebrews 13:4 AMP

My wife and I have wonderful intimacy, yet we know this
isn't the reality in many Christian marriages—because the
enemy is sabotaging them. Marriage and intimacy are honorable, but Satan can gain access to your bedroom if you aren't
handling sex in a godly way. Sadly, the church often isn't comfortable dealing with the real issues, so divorce statistics for
Christian couples are skyrocketing.

Sexual enticement and perversion are rampant in our society. Everywhere you turn, people are doing things exactly the
opposite of what God intended. So how can we expect Him to
bless our love? What's the truth about making love from a bib-
lical perspective? Come with me to the Song of Solomon.

The fig tree puts forth and ripens her green figs, and the vines are in blossom and give forth their fragrance. Arise, my love, my fair one, and come away. [So I went with him, and when we were climbing the rocky steps up the hillside, my beloved shepherd said to me] O my dove, [while you are here] in the seclusion of the clefts in the solid rock, in the sheltered and secret place of the cliff, let me see your face, let me hear your voice; for your voice is sweet, and your face is lovely. [My heart was touched and I fervently sang to him my desire] Take for us the foxes, the little foxes that spoil the vineyards [of our love], for our vineyards are in blossom. [She said distinctly] My beloved is mine and I am his! He pastures his flocks among the lilies (2:13–16 AMP).

This reveals God has a right time, place, and way for husbands and wives to guard passion in their marriages. Therefore, we must embrace His wisdom and deal with the issues that can spoil our romance. Let me explain. *Taking the little foxes* means to seize and hold in our possession the little things that dig at the substance of our love, perverting the beauty of what God has created for us to enjoy (Strong's, #H270, #H7776/#H8168, #H6996, #H2254, #H3754/#H5563). This means we have no choice but to identify the real issues about sex—because the enemy will start trying to kill your intimacy from the time your love begins to bloom.

Notice a strong parallel is drawn between Solomon's encounter and a believer's intimacy with God. Moses was hidden in the cleft of a rock on Mount Sinai while the glory of God passed over him (Exodus 33:19–23). He received the commandments, ordinances, and instructions for the temple on that mountain (Exodus 19:20–31:18). Psalm 91 says those who dwell in God's *"secret place"* will abide in His shadow and be kept safe from evil. *The secret place is where you see God's face and hear His voice.* Oh, yes! The marriage bed is holy.

This also reveals that it takes great effort to develop and protect marital intimacy. Solomon and his love had to *climb the rocky steps* to reach their destination. In the Hebrew, *stairs* means "a steep or inaccessible place" (Strong's, #H4095). If you've ever climbed a mountain, you understand it takes a lot of physical effort, balance, and stamina to make it to the top. And the higher you go, the harder it is to breathe, because the oxygen pressure is lower at high altitudes. In short, you can't reach the heights of intimacy in your marriage without God— because this level of relationship is so sacred, it reflects His glory. And when flesh comes in contact with the glory of God, it must be covered, or it will fail. You need a *threefold cord* to keep your marriage bed intact (see Ecclesiastes 4:11–12).

One more revelation...the maiden's shepherd led her to the rocky steps. So first, understand that Jesus is going to lead you directly to *secret places* that have been difficult for you to handle. And if you follow His path of wisdom, you can overcome each one of them. Second, I believe a husband can help his wife in this process. Many times God will use a man to draw out painful, intimate memories in a woman so they can be healed. So, brother, always remember, *lead through love.*

Let Go of the Past

Let's start with things you've experienced prior to marriage. If you dated ten people before you got married, chances are that issues from at least five of these relationships will follow you into the marriage. Some of these wounds can be dangerous. How? *Because you think you've gotten over them.* And when they resurface, you're blindsided. *Little foxes.* Listen to me. Just because a person's no longer in your life doesn't mean he or she can't affect your marriage.

Both Juanita and I had to deal with romantic issues from the past. And notice I say *deal with* because there's a tendency to avoid them, hold it in, and pray—*but never confront.* That's when enticement really gets a foothold—because you're not letting go of something that touched you in the fleshly realm. Think about it. Have you ever said, "Kiss me right here..." or "Hold me like this…"? Why did you want your wife to kiss you there? Why did you want your husband to hold you like that? It could be your flesh trying to remember something from the past.

You need to admit you have these issues and take them to God in repentance. Then let Him help you to be honest with your partner. Say honestly, "Listen, I don't know if this will be an issue with you, but I need to get free from the memory of…" If you don't identify these things, the enemy will try to entice you with the prospect that you could have them again. And as soon as you get into a conversational difficulty, your flesh will say, "I could have somebody else kiss me, hug me, or love me the way I really like it." *Little foxes!*

An interesting issue resurfaced in me once when Juanita and I were talking about our marriage plans (just so you know, we got married privately and then planned a public celebration to take place several months later). She said, "Honey, I really want you to look good for our wedding day." "No problem," I said. "I really want to get in the gym myself."

Thank God, *I know me.* I had gone to the gym regularly while I was separated in my first relationship, so I knew I'd be in real trouble if Juanita didn't help me. Up until the time of her request, I had suppressed going to the gym because there was no way I could work myself up, wake up my body, and have nobody to hold at night. So I said to her, "I'd love to be in great shape—but if that's the case, you and I need to be with each other a little bit more than we are now." That's when she surprised me and took a whole day off for us to be alone during a week-long revival. Don't you know how fast I locked that door? I would have been in bad shape if she'd greeted me saying, "Oh…hi, honey. How are you? Get your suit on, we're going to church."

Believe me, honesty can save you a lot of trouble in your relationship. Instead of suffering from enticement, I talked to my wife…and she ministered to my need.

Here's another thing about dealing with the past. During conversational difficulties, your flesh always wants to be comforted when God's trying to purify your spirit toward your spouse. When issues come to the surface, see it as God trying to heal you. Take the divine opportunity to reach higher heights of intimacy in your marriage. Make yourself vulnerable…*tell the truth in love.* Too many people give in to the flesh and say, "You know what, maybe I made a mistake here. I need to make sure that I really love this person, for he's not who I thought he was."

Love can be very strange. Don't bring old baggage into a new relationship. You and your spouse have enough work ahead of you climbing that mountain by yourselves. When Jesus was teaching John's disciples about fasting, He said,

> *And no one puts a piece of cloth that has not been shrunk on an old garment, for such a patch tears away from the garment and a worse rent (tear) is made. Neither is new wine put in old wineskins; for if it is, the skins burst and are torn in pieces, and the wine is spilled and the skins are ruined. But new wine is put into fresh wineskins, and so both are preserved* (Matthew 9:16–17 AMP).

Do you see the revelation? Don't carry the old into the new. Deal with past issues. Go into your marriage with a fresh perspective, and God will preserve your passion.

Developing Your Intimate Relationship

Communication is a must. And again, I believe the man is able to initiate this process by allowing his wife to discern his passion. As time goes on, she becomes more and more free in expressing her passionate needs. For a man, sex is physical; but for a woman, it's an emotional act—so give her time to embrace the fullness of your passion. Above all else, learn to be honest with each other. Brother, find out if she likes corn chips or potato chips with sour cream and onions. Sister, maybe he really likes barbeque. I'm trying to be delicate, but it's vital that each of you shares what you desire while keeping your partner's pleasure in mind.

Sister, let me say this as well. A man doesn't understand a woman's need when he constantly gives her the same thing he's been giving her the last two, three, five, or ten years…*because a woman's never the same.* Men get into routines. So you need to tell your husband, "I don't want a routine. I want romance!" Romance is definitely not routine; it's always surprising your partner with something new. Romance is doing something different…something the other person wasn't expecting. *Tell him.* Encourage him to explore.

When it comes to your sensual needs, help your husband to understand the *real you*—not the part of you that sings in the choir. Believe me, when you're together, he's not expecting you to sing the "Hallelujah Chorus"! In fact, he'll like it best when you're saying and doing things that don't seem spiritual at all. Your marriage bed is undefiled, so there's grace for what you do there. It's the place where you can become uninhibited in all of the areas you've been guarded: emotionally, psychologically, and (most importantly) sexually.

A truly godly husband will ask what your sexual appetite is, then protect you by not advancing beyond where you're comfortable—*because he really wants to experience the truth of who you are.*

This leads to another level of intimacy, for a man needs to *experience* what a woman *communicates.* In other words, a husband needs to be taught how to have foreplay. And sister, one way you can help him is by learning to transition him out of one mode and into another. Let me explain. A man will always know that you're introducing something new when you change visualization. Oh, yes! Get a few items from Victoria's Secret or another intimate apparel store. Show him what you're in the mood to receive.

By changing your husband's visual reference, you're introducing him to a new role. If you put on shorts and a tee shirt, you're telling him it's summertime. If you put on a fur coat, hat, and gloves, you're telling him it's wintertime. If you put on lingerie, you're telling him it's sex time. You're saying to him, "I want to be treated like a sexual woman."

You need to introduce foreplay and sensuality because your husband doesn't need foreplay to get excited about loving you. He only needs thought play. He simply needs to think about sex, and his body begins to respond. And brother, your wife needs to hear and feel. That's why she likes a warm, inviting atmosphere where the lights are turned down low.

Let's explore this a little further. A woman is like an old-fashioned copper kettle. It takes a few minutes for the water to come to a boil, but once it gets hot, it stays hot for a long, long time. (In copper pots, water stays warm for about one and a half to two hours because they're made to hold the temperature.) And when you've really awakened her, you can enjoy the first cup of tea, go back an hour later for another cup, and then again another hour later for a third cup of tea.

So, sister, you must let your husband know, "I'm not a tin pot; I'm copper. I have the capacity to hold affection and keep it warm until you're ready for the next cup." *When a man understands you're not a one-cup kettle, he'll enjoy the process of warming you up.* You can teach him by telling him, but you've got to train him by providing the experience, for a man doesn't know how to be your lover. He only knows how to give you love. If your partner regularly does something you don't enjoy, it's probably because you haven't told him exactly how you like it.

Please don't miss this because a man can love you without giving you what you need. For example, if he's seen his father "loving" his mother by yelling at her, he thinks that's love. This means sexual communication is vital. You have to teach your husband how you need to be loved—because every man has been introduced to love by watching some other male in his life, whether it was his father, uncle, cousin, or friend.

Now back to you, brother. Understanding that your wife is a copper kettle, you need to work at building endurance. A woman will always try to endure longer than you because she's made that way. If you understand how to take care of yourself and do the things that need to be done, you can endure to the end…because that's what your wife really needs. And sister, if your man can't endure, get him to the gym, give him vitamins, get him on herbal products; do whatever it takes to boost his stamina.

I can't close without saying this: When a man becomes selfish, it's always proven in his sexuality. He won't make sure you're rewarded the way you ought to be during lovemaking. Once your husband understands how you need to be loved, he should never leave you unrewarded, no matter what it takes to give you that reward. Now that's a godly husband.

Don't Withhold Your Love

Every marriage has conversational difficulties. And when they come, there's a temptation to react and let that separate you. Please hear me…don't let it happen. Let's read 1 Corinthians 7:3–6 in the Amplified Bible:

> *The husband should give to his wife her conjugal rights (goodwill, kindness, and what is due her as his wife), and likewise the wife to her husband. For the wife does not have [exclusive] authority and control*

*over her own body, but the husband [has his rights];
likewise also the husband does not have [exclusive]
authority and control over his body, but the wife
[has her rights]. Do not refuse and deprive and de-
fraud each other [of your due marital rights], except
perhaps by mutual consent for a time, so that you
may devote yourselves unhindered to prayer. But afterwards resume marital relations, lest Satan tempt
you [to sin] through your lack of restraint of sexual
desire. But I am saying this more as a matter of permission and concession, not as a command or
regulation.*

When a woman is upset, especially if she has a strong
temperament, she'll pull back from the intimate experience.
For her, it's an emotional issue; but as a husband, you must lead
her through love. If not, she'll stretch you out on a limb until
you acknowledge her. And she won't give in until you break.
Sister, if you struggle with this, let your husband help you—
because withholding lovemaking is the most dangerous thing
you can do. If you love God and truly want to minister to your
husband's needs, you won't try to control him this way.

Don't break this trust with your husband, for it could be
difficult for you to get it back. The temptation caused by un-
willing celibacy could bring disaster in your home. *Don't let
little foxes spoil your vine.* Be angry, but don't fall into sin.
Don't let the sun go down on your wrath. If you do, you'll give
place to the devil (Ephesians 4:26–27).

Brother, the same holds true for you. Don't starve your
wife of affection! If you're mad because she didn't cook your
meal, and then she puts on a negligee, you'd better give her the

love she needs. Listen. The enemy can really mess you up here, and you'll start playing games with your wife. Believe me, it's worse when your wife is ready for love and you say you're not feeling it tonight.

You need to be on your job before and after your wife comes around for that month. Go work out and get plenty of rest. If she comes to you and says, "Honey, can we spend a couple of days together?" And you respond, "Well, Sam's supposed to come over and help me build that shed in the back, and it's going to take a couple of days..." That's wrong, and it's definitely not wisdom. She's trying to let you know that she needs you. Don't break her trust in you.

Juanita and I talk. One or the other of us will say, "All right, baby, let me look at the calendar. Okay, nothing else is going to happen two days before or two days after." My wife feels the liberty to tell me, "Honey, you need to be prepared—because I'm going to be a wild woman." And I'm always ready to respond, "Okay, you be a wild woman. My middle name is Tarzan."

Don't Fall into a Deadly Trap

Let me start by saying the Bible doesn't condone adultery (Hebrews 13:4). Yet, understand that the Scriptures also clearly say a man or woman can cause their spouse to fall into temptation if they withhold marital relations for too long. It's one thing to have a conversational difficulty and eventually work through it. It's entirely another to routinely withhold affection from your partner. And when this starts happening, temptation is imminent.

I'll begin with the man's perspective. When he loves his wife and trusts her with all that he has, it can be very damaging to him if she constantly rejects him. What can actually start happening is he slowly begins to take a portion of his love and put it somewhere else. A man never wants to feel like he's being rejected from embracing a woman who belongs to him. That's why Juanita and I constantly work at our ability to embrace each other completely. We're not going to let Satan get close to establishing a foothold.

When a wife rejects her husband, he can then be tempted by something I refer to as *the silent wife* (i.e., the other woman). You see, when a wife can't submit to her husband, she eventually tries to control him in other ways…and it usually ends up in the bedroom. That's when enticement kicks in. Since she won't embrace him, he begins to reflect on how he used to get comfort from other women whenever he sensed rejection. *Little foxes*.

Then the silent wife enters, and the interesting thing is, it doesn't have to be a sexual thing. She could simply be somebody your husband feels he can talk to—the friend who hears and encourages him, "Don't worry, it's going to get better." This type of relationship seems to be innocent, but it's extremely dangerous…because *silent beginnings* usually end in seduction. Brother, if your marriage is in turmoil, embrace wisdom…run to God, *not to another woman*. Jesus said if you look at another woman with desire in your heart, the damage has already been done (Matthew 5:27–28). So don't look, *and definitely don't go*.

This enticement is lethal. If you go to another woman when your wife rejects you, your flesh actually gets excited—because when you're with the silent wife, you don't sense rejection. You feel love…*but it isn't the truth.* You're being enticed by her quietness. She doesn't have to make the sacrifices to be your wife, so she can hear the same things you say to your wife without reacting. After all, she doesn't have to be committed to help you change. It's very easy to embrace that.

Let me offer a little bit of wisdom. Many times a silent wife doesn't want to be the woman she is. Sometimes she can't help but love you because she sees your pain. She automatically loves, so when she finds something to love in you, she'll get attached. So flee from temptation, man of God, because if you fall, you won't be able to retrieve the love you gave her. After she starts loving you, you can't ever get it back—because in her spirit, she'll be following you wherever you go. When you go home, her silent spirit will still be with you. And while you're trying to encourage love with your wife, she'll be sensing your need in another place.

Just for argument's sake, let's say this woman isn't so satisfied. She'll be thinking, "I'm glad you're not my husband. As soon as I can, I'm ending this relationship." Then a few weeks later, she comes and tells you, "I'm seeing somebody else." Now you've got dual rejection—and it sends you into a tailspin. You thought you had someone to embrace, but it was a lie. A silent wife can't heal you. A real wife can…but like you, she needs time to grow.

The truth is, a real wife will never ask you to do more than you're able to do. She just wants you to do something that says, "I love you."

So, sister, never reject your husband, for when a woman sees a real man, she'll start submitting…even if he belongs to somebody else. (That's why the Bible tells wives to submit to *their own* husbands [Ephesians 5:22; Colossians 3:18].) And when another woman starts submitting to your husband, you're going to have a fight on your hands. If she gets half of him, she'll want the other half. Eventually, she'll be calling you saying, "I don't know why you're trying to hold onto him while I've got all of him." Then it escalates into a fatal attraction, and somebody's going to get hurt.

Sister, if you're angry with your husband, ask God to help you deal with your pain. Instead of controlling him through passion, try embracing and releasing him into the love of God. *The truth is, a man gets confused when he's rejected because, to him, actions demonstrate love.*

Let me explain. When a man can't deal with his pain, he'll come to you silently trying to reach for your compassion. However, if you're hurting and can't embrace his pain, he'll become vulnerable. Granted, he may not deserve your affection at that moment, but if you can give him what he needs, he won't become vulnerable to an enticing spirit.

If you're going to bruise the head of Satan, sister, then you need to start by killing rejection. You really need to help your husband in this area because, from a revelational perspective, *he was rejected out of the Garden*. That's why men have an innate reaction to rejection. So when you reject him, he feels death, shame, and bitter remorse. When a woman rejects a man, it awakens a natural emotion in him that stems from the Adamic part of his soul.

So it's not that he doesn't love you; he just couldn't find love when he needed you. Now let me clarify again—*it's wrong to have an affair*—but it's definitely wise to be *real*. As his wife, know that he'll come to you even when you're upset because you have something that he needs more than his pain. And if you can meet his need (even though you're both hurting), you'll never have to worry about a *silent wife*.

Hear me, sister. You have the power to keep love in your marriage.

It's a different situation when a woman is enticed. And what usually causes this to happen is a husband's irresponsibility. When a man starts forgetting her basic needs, it literally drives a woman crazy—because she doesn't ask for a lot right away. She just asks him to give her the essentials. If this is you, brother—watch out! *The foxes are coming....*

Here's how it plays out. The husband comes home from work, sits down, and starts watching television. The whole time, she's been trying to get his attention. She's not asking him for much; she just wants to hug and say *hello*. He's frozen in front of the television set, flipping the channels. So he turns and says, "Baby, I'll be with you in five minutes...I just have to catch this."

To her, it's not about "five minutes" anymore. It's about five minutes that will lead to five hours, and *that* five hours has already been accumulating daily for five weeks! *And she's still trying to get his attention.* Before long, she starts saying to herself, *There's something wrong with this man. He's not taking care of business like he should, and he's not taking care of our home.* Finally, after he's exhausted all of his chances, she starts playing games with him. *Little foxes are spoiling the vines.*

Hear me, brother. The worst thing for a woman to feel is rejection when all she wants is to be embraced. She's trying to tell you, "I'm going through something in my emotions that I need to feel secure in. I'm going through a struggle with my esteem, and I need you to give your confidence to me. I don't understand why a television program has more power over you than I do. I don't understand why hanging with your friends always seems to be more important...you schedule things *with them* two weeks in advance, but you forget the things I need."

Let me pause here. Men tend to schedule activities out of emotional desire, but they're not tapped into a woman's emotional need. So a husband's priorities become an issue of *his desire* versus *her need*. And when a man desires to do something, he'll remember to do it.

Let's return to the scenario. Two weeks later, the husband puts on his coat and goes off to enjoy the game with the guys. At the same time, his wife leaves for the mall to deal with her frustration by shopping. She's on her way to buy something that embraces her emotions and says, *"I love you."*

While she's there, an attractive, single man notices her. And as she walks by, he takes the opportunity to tell her that he appreciates what he sees. She stops, turns around, and says, "Thank you so much." Then he responds, "I'm going over to the Food Court. Are you hungry?" *"I'm a little thirsty..."* They walk and talk all the way.

Now they begin to find commonality, "Oh, you like lemonade? I know the best lemonade...so-and-so has the best..." and he's showing her the money in his wallet. "What else do you want?" They leave the lemonade stand and stroll to the other side of the mall to find some items she's been wanting. So while her husband is at the game, rooting with the guys, she's being charmed by a man who sees her potential. And the scene continues to unfold. *She gets a little cold, he gives her his coat...and so on.*

So while her husband thinks she's out getting stockings, she's actually getting something else. He comes back home, and she makes sure to come back with a shopping bag in her hands—because she can't act like she didn't shop all day. Then while she's putting things away, he suddenly jumps up and wants some attention. She shoots a glare at him as if to say, "Why are you looking at me now? You didn't want me before." Then she walks off to the other side of the house. And the man is clueless.

So he starts tripping and thinks, "Fine...no problem with me," and returns to his chair to embrace the television. He doesn't realize that she's slipped off to call the other man, "You know, I really enjoyed this afternoon; it was really special, but listen...I have to tell you the truth. I'm married." *"I know,"* he says, *"no problem."* Then the enticement continues to build. She asks, "Can you meet me after work? I work at such-and-such a place...*I'll call you.*"

This is when she starts acting like she doesn't care if she sees her husband. She lays out her clothes and goes to bed early because she wants her beauty rest. Then she gets up early the next day and rushes off to work. And since her husband has lost sensitivity to her needs, he's still thinking he can "click it on" and "click it off" whenever he wants. *The truth of the matter is, he needs to develop the capacity to sow time and attention into his wife.*

The other man knows how to treat a woman right every day. And this speaks to her rejection issue. She's been trying to communicate to her husband, "I want to be treated right every day, and if you only want to treat me like your wife when you want sex, then we're going to have serious problems." Interestingly, the other man doesn't have to give her money. He only needs to give her the attention she's not getting at home. And as she gets more attention from him, it starts turning into affection…and affection leads to everything else. *The vines of love have been spoiled.*

How can this husband win back his wife? He must learn how to repent of his ignorance. When she comes back home, he needs to have flowers in his hand. And he must be prepared to apologize and admit that he's been wrong. If he really loves her, he'll confess, "Listen, it was my fault. I'm the one who messed up."

Deep in her heart, his wife really desires his affection. The other man was just somebody who filled a need. Unfortunately, their ungodly soul tie has released that man to live inside of her. So she might accept your flowers, but not your love. She has to denounce his name in order to put your name back on the throne of her heart.

Brother, if your name isn't on the throne of your wife's heart, you're not loved…*you're getting faked out*. If you take your wife for granted, ask for forgiveness; but realize things might be a little stuffy for a while if you allowed her to become attached to somebody else. And really, she didn't want it to happen—she was just uncovered by you, *her lord*.

Remember, when a woman sees God in you, she's automatically attracted to the God inside of your spirit. So, brother, please don't take God off the throne in your heart, for if you do, your wife could start submitting to another God in another man. The God *in you* must be the God that she serves…not the one that beats her up, curses her out, uses and manipulates her, and then tramples on her love.

If you don't have a good sex life, you won't have a great saved life. It's time to get real about sex because what the church has been afraid to talk about, the devil has been taking full advantage of. *Take (seize) the little foxes* that are trying to spoil the fruit of your love. Let wisdom wash your spirit, and endure God's process in your marriage. *Protect the intimate gift God has given you.* Your bed is undefiled.

III

Beginning a New Heritage

God's Wisdom for Establishing Your Home

> I was confident that God had called me to be her husband.
> And I understood that I would need to make the sacrifice…
> –TWW

- Letting wisdom build your house
- Breaking the power of contention
- Overcoming the pain of broken promises
- Coming into divine balance

Strength and dignity are her clothing and her position is strong and secure; she rejoices over the future [the latter day or time to come, knowing that she and her family are in readiness for it]!
Proverbs 31:25 AMP

CHAPTER 7

SISTER, DON'T HURT A BROTHER

Every wise woman builds her house,
but the foolish one tears it down with her own hands.
Proverbs 14:1 AMP

A man can always tell what a woman is feeling by what she does with her hands. If she's angry, she folds them. If she's a little aggravated, she'll put them on her hips. If she wants to be direct, she'll point her finger in his face. And if she's in love with him, she'll reach out to him in gentleness. A woman's hands always indicate her emotional level.

One day while talking about our wedding, I told Juanita, "Let's do something a little different. When we exchange rings, I want you to wear your diamond on your left hand and your marriage band on your right hand." According to some Jewish friends of ours, in Hebrew custom the woman's power is expressed through her right hand and her love for the family through her left. So when rings are placed on a woman's hands in marriage, they're both covered in the relationship.

When I shared this with Juanita, she said, "That's strange, because I was already seeing that." And I said, "Yes, and I really want you to consider this distinctive aspect of Hebrew culture.

As your husband, I'm going to cover you in both of your hands. So you'll always be covered in the balance of who you are."

How Does a Wise Woman Build?

What is it about a wise woman that gives her the ability to build, where a foolish woman plucks down with her own hands? Let me start by saying a wise woman never operates out of her emotions. She knows they're unstable, so she's learned to embrace God and her husband. A wise woman has learned to appreciate *the covering.* Let's go back to Proverbs 14:1:

> *Every wise woman builds her house, but the foolish one tears it down with her own hands* (AMP).

In Hebrew, *hands* indicate *power*, *means*, and *direction* (Strong's, #H3027). So from a revelational perspective, this communicates a wise woman is full of faith and vision. She understands her anointing, purpose, and spiritual assignment in her family. Take Juanita, for example. She firmly believes a virtuous wife should always be in the position to receive a word from the Lord for her husband—because she rises *"while it is yet night"* to get *"spiritual food"* for her household (Proverbs 31:15 AMP). A wise woman understands that God must build the house *through* her (Psalm 127:1). She's submitted and faithful in her home.

A virtuous woman is focused on releasing the potential in *her* home, *not* everybody else's. She's not trying to assimilate what "Sarah" did next door—she's building her own house according to her ability in God.

Sister, when you're constantly trying to get confirmation about how to handle your issues from another woman in another house, you'll never be able to build your home. For example, if you always vent your feelings to Sarah and then ask what she thinks you should do about your marriage, finances, children, and so on—I have news for you; you're not building your house. You're building *Sarah*, and *she's* building your house.

Sarah may be offering good advice, but she doesn't live in your house! She doesn't have an anointing to build your family. She's simply trying to be a friend and respond to what you're saying. It isn't possible for Sarah to have a real understanding of the issues in your home *because she's not you.* The truth is, God's trying to deal with her about her own house. Proverbs 31:27 says,

> *She looks well to how things go in her household, and the bread of idleness (gossip, discontent, and self-pity) she will not eat* (AMP)

This reveals an important truth: If you have time to sit and talk with Sarah, something's not getting done at home. You're idle. So you start seeing every little detail you don't like and multiplying each one with your friend. Then she echoes your feelings and you feel justified. No, you're foolish…but I'll get to that later.

Also, I don't understand why some women go to somebody who hasn't built her house to ask how they should build theirs. It amazes me how women who are about to get married go to their single friends for advice. Listen, your friend may love God—but can she know how to build a family? That's not wisdom. The Bible says mature, holy women are to teach the young how to love their families and keep their homes in order (Titus 2:3–5).

When people enter a wise woman's house, they're not walking into a shell with a color scheme and furniture. They're entering a place where she nurtures life. They're coming into an atmosphere where her presence can be felt in every room. God has anointed her to impart wisdom and life to all who enter that place,

> *She opens her mouth in skillful and godly Wisdom, and on her tongue is the law of kindness [giving counsel and instruction]* (Proverbs 31:26 AMP).

Sister, if you let God use you to build your house, He'll give you a powerful anointing in whatever you do. Everything in your hands will prosper.

Whose House Is It Anyway?

Now, brother, most likely you already know your home *really* belongs to your wife. You live there, *but it's hers.* You may pay the mortgage, but it's not your house. Here's a spiritual secret...*every wise woman builds her house, and a wise man builds his wife.* The husband's house is the woman. And if he builds the woman, she'll build the house. This is why problems spring up when a man is trying to build the house *and not* his wife. She feels "vacated"...and the home becomes empty.

Here's the truth: If you're really building your wife, you shouldn't mind that it's her house...*because you're the king of her heart.* She'll do everything with you in mind. As she goes about her day, she'll be thinking of pleasing you and making you happy. How could you have a problem with that? Learn to celebrate the fact that the physical house will never be yours.

Your wife has been uniquely anointed to create an atmosphere and continuity in your home. For example, men can really mess things up. We'll put on plaid pants, a solid shirt, and a faded cap, and think we're looking good! Then our wife will come along and say, "Oh no, no, no…honey, that's not going to work." She'll bring that chaos into balance; she's just built that way.

Think about bachelors. Most usually have two colors in their house, typically black and white. Men generally don't deal with a lot of colors, so light shades or pastels are likely to be absent in a place he's put together. The majority of bachelors don't like spending time painting, either…*or* cleaning up. Like it or not, men just don't have the same anointing God has imparted to women—but when a woman's building a house, her husband can see the need…and will help her any way he can.

Let me say it again. A woman's gift is to build her house—but a man's gift is to build the woman. And whatever he builds *in her* gets built into the house where he rests. When you think about this, brother, what's so bad about helping with the laundry or cleaning up a few dishes? If you'll give her what she needs, you'll receive what you need from her and more.

If a man is selfish, he won't build his wife. Then he'll end up wondering why the house isn't in order. Truthfully, a man gets blinded about building his wife because he's usually building his car. It can become almost like a *silent wife* to him. Generally speaking, I think at least seventy-five to eighty percent of all men put more attention into their cars than they do their wives. They'll make sure the gas tank is filled before trying to make their wives happy. They'll take care of everything concerning their transportation while the wife has to struggle to be emotionally satisfied.

Men will buy new air fresheners and stick them under the front seat, but they won't bring something new and fresh into the marriage. Why? A man typically spends the majority of his time in his car. And he usually does this because he hasn't taken the time to build his wife. Brother, if you'll build your wife, she'll build the house, and the house will become a place of restoration for you. If you're willing to invest in your wife, she'll make her house your home.

I've been down the road a few times when it comes to buying houses. The other day, I told my wife, "I think I'm ready to buy another house…" and then I took her to see it. As we were walking through, she was coming up with great ideas. *Then I saw a room that I liked.* So I turned to her and said, "If you don't mind, do you think I could have this room over here? I'll give you the rest of the house…" I was really negotiating.

We had a wonderful conversation about the room, but then Juanita saw another one that she liked even better for me—the office. She walked in, sat down, and said, "Baby, this is a nice office and library; this is perfect for you. God, this is just wonderful…you can walk outside…and just look at all the shelf space."

I said, "Yeah, that's great. I like it," but I really wanted the other room downstairs. I was trying to be wise; I didn't want to quench her excitement. She wanted me to consider the office, and her reasoning made sense, so I'm continuing to pray. And to be honest, if I don't get the first room I wanted, I'm not going to get bent out of shape about it. I understand my greatest room is *in her.*

This is how it works. If I take care of the room *in my wife*, she'll automatically take care of the physical room I want to be mine.

This reminds me of a young couple who came to counsel with me. They were so excited about getting married and having children right away. I tried to convince them otherwise. "Would you please find jobs before having a child?" Sadly, they couldn't be dissuaded. "No, the Lord called us to get married, and He's going to give us a child." Sure enough, she got pregnant. After the baby came, they didn't have enough money to provide for the child and had to deal with a lot of serious issues.

I had pleaded with them, "You don't need to get married and have a baby right away. Why don't you get married, work hard, and put some money aside? Live for a little while." Sometimes the issue may be a husband is trying to build something, even though his wife isn't ready for it—and because she loves him, she tries to submit. Let me shed some light on this: A wise woman would have said to her foolish husband, "We can't have children right now. I don't care how much you love children, honey, this isn't the time. We're not prepared for it."

Jesus said, *"Ye are the salt of the earth: but if the salt have lost his savour, wherewith shall it be salted? it is thenceforth good for nothing, but to be cast out, and to be trodden under foot of men"* (Matthew 5:13). Sister, God has seasoned you to make a difference in your home. If you lose your savor, or anointing, in the home…you won't be able to truly help your husband. Don't let the enemy compromise your purpose.

Love your husband enough to be honest and tell him about what God is speaking to your heart. How else can you help him build a strong future for your family? And husband, be strong enough to receive sound wisdom from your wife. Recognize her anointing in the home, and then take the matter to God. If she's right, He'll confirm it and help you to make a wise decision.

A Wise Woman Creates an Atmosphere for Her Husband

Sister, the atmosphere of your home should call to your husband. So if he never seems to be at home, something's wrong. You must create an atmosphere that makes him feel welcomed. I've known many people with a lot of money in the bank, yet the woman didn't know how to make her house their home. How much you have isn't really important—it's what you do with it, and the spirit you release in your home, that count.

Let's look at the practical side. A man needs to have a specific place in the home where he feels he can get some R&R—a football or sports room perhaps. He needs a television and a couch where he can lay low and eat potato chips…because this is how he's built. Create an environment that's just for him, and he'll always come home *because that room is there.*

Here's a secret for you: If you can get him home and make *that* room right for him, then you can have the *other room* right for the *other thing*…do you understand? When your husband comes out of one season in his room, another season could kick in for both of you in the secret place.

Set up an environment where your husband can feel, "This is my domain." Granted, it's your house, but you have to give him *some space* that's actually *his.* If you have children, don't let them go into his special environment. Say, "Junior, you stay out; that's daddy's area right there. Don't move the remote; let it stay where he left it. And leave the television alone."

The worse thing in the world for a man is to come home, turn on the television, and see cartoons jump onto the screen. It's an immediate reminder that he's not going to have any peace tonight. Let him come home and unwind a bit—greet him with a kiss, tell him how much you love him, and then give him a little time in his special place. Make his homecoming memorable; then he'll start looking forward to relaxing *in you* first. You won't ever have to compete with the evening news when you teach him that his first and best room is *in you*.

Let's say you have a two-bedroom apartment. You can still set up a little space somewhere, even in the bedroom. Let me tell you, sister, if you make room for your man, he'll be happy to spend time there—especially when you see to it his favorite snacks are close by. You know what I'm saying—cheese curls, potato chips and dip, ginger ale—*whatever he likes*. Keep them in a cupboard that only he has access to.

Little things mean a lot. My mom was really good at this. I can still hear her saying, "Listen, this cupboard is for you and your brother. Whatever's in *this* cupboard is yours." There were Oreo cookies and other snacks for us to enjoy—but my father had the wheat thins in his cupboard, which was above the refrigerator. There was no way we could ever say we'd made a mistake and reached in there.

Every now and then after dinner, he'd go over and open up his cabinet. And I have to admit, my brother and I felt deprived—because we didn't have the *little wheat things*. One day, my dad was feeling generous and decided to leave the remainder of a box on the counter for my brother and me. We devoured it and wanted more. So we went into his cupboard and got another box. Believe me, he noticed. "Leona, what happened to my box?" Of course, my brother and I played dumb, but we could not deny it.

The point is, a wise woman knows how to create a special environment for the man she loves. There were even items in our refrigerator that my brother and I couldn't touch. My father never ate pork; he always ate beef bacon. On the other hand, my mother loved pork, but she'd cook beef bacon *just for him*—so he felt like a king. Every now and then, he'd let us have a little piece of his bacon. And then there was the peach cobbler…we never had it unless my father asked for it. My mother didn't make cobbler for the family. She'd say, "Honey, this is your peach cobbler." And dad would say, "Give the boys a little pinch of it."

A wise woman knows how to separate what should belong to her husband from what belongs to everybody else. And there needs to be some definition because, from a spiritual perspective, separating something makes it distinctive. And when there's no distinctiveness in a relationship, there can't be any excitement—because nothing's been set apart as being special. Sister, don't think about this in a worldly way. Embrace the fact that you'll minister life to your husband when you treat him like a king.

A Wise Woman Multiplies Her Home

A woman's hands have a unique anointing; she's got a survival mechanism that's not built into a man. Let's say a woman has $200. She can make it last twice as long as a man. She has innate radar when it comes to catching sales and saving money.

A man can go to fifteen different places and never find what he's looking for, but a woman has a gut instinct that's like a built-in GPS system. When a sale for something she needs is within a certain radius, lights start flashing.

My mother could make anything work, whether we had a little or a lot. While my family was living in South Bend, Indiana, there were heavy snowstorms that dropped a minimum of fourteen to twenty-five inches at a time. In 1976, we got snowed in for two weeks by a blizzard that relentlessly dropped fifty-four inches of snow in four days—the snowdrifts were over seven-and-a-half feet high. We couldn't see any cars on the street; they were buried beneath the snow. As a matter of fact, I can remember not being able to see other houses.

It took us two weeks to shovel out and get back to normal. I remember attaching cardboard to our feet and walking three miles to the supermarket (and of course everybody was trying to get the little bit of food that was left). My mother purchased a few things and made them last for almost a week and a half, until we could actually get back to the supermarket. She got a little bit of Bisquick, some eggs, a little bit of milk, butter, and so on. We had biscuits, pancakes, this and that—all from a box of powder.

Now I understand how my father was able to rest in her anointing to multiply. He didn't have to worry that his children would be hungry, cold, or without any good thing. A wise woman has a powerful anointing in her home. She's a master builder. That's why her family rises up and calls her blessed (Proverbs 31:28).

Let me repeat a worthy thought for you, brother. When you really love your wife and want to spend more time with her, you'll help around the house—even if you have to hire somebody every now and then. Take time with your wife; build her up and give her what she needs. Take her out and show her a really good time; it tells her you care. *And remember*, care leads to affection. Steal her away for a weekend whenever you can. Tell her, "I just have to be with you…" Pay somebody to cut the grass. Do whatever you can to let her know, "You're my house."

A Foolish Woman Lives out of Her Emotions

A foolish woman plucks down what God is trying to build. She operates by how she feels instead of by what she knows in her spirit. In the Hebrew, *foolish* means silly or perverse (Strong's, #H200/#H191). In other words, sister, if you don't embrace wisdom for your home—if you refuse to build your house—*you're in disobedience to God*. You're following your emotions and doing exactly the opposite of what He's created you to do. Don't you think that's silly?

Feelings can be deceptive, and I'll explain why. Your emotions are based on past experiences. So when a new thought enters your mind, your emotions immediately attach meaning to it. This is why you have to become wise in the counsel of the Lord. His Word has *power* to *renew* your mind and keep your emotions in check (Hebrew 4:12; Romans 12:2). This is why a wise woman rises at night to get *spiritual food* for her household (Proverbs 31:15). It's the best time for her to be still before God and receive what she needs to be a virtuous woman.

A prayerless woman becomes foolish and starts destroying what she's supposed to build. Let me explain. A foolish woman speaks negatively about what God has created to be positive. She starts discussing things with people who can't keep their mouths shut…and they turn it into her downfall. Sister, be very careful to avoid doing this. Don't hurt your husband because he has some negative qualities. Make sure your hands are committed to building his life, and God will continue building you.

For a woman, there's no middle ground; you'll either be emotionally attached to living or unemotionally attached to existing. A foolish woman merely exists in her environment. She becomes coarse toward her husband and ineffective in her home. When he tries to touch her, she's unresponsive—she just wants to get it over with. A foolish woman becomes cordial, *not congenial*. She's soft, but not sassy. In short, she's not living anymore. Emotionally, she's pulled herself out, so that she doesn't exist in her emotions.

The dangerous thing is what I call "shut down." When a woman goes into shut down, it's like a nuclear reactor that kicks into emergency mode. In order to reset the reactor, the technicians have to put on protective gear and be quarantined in a radiation tank. Then they can go to the next level and realign the nuclear fusion and uranium core (before reactivating the plant). This is a tedious process because they actually have to remove and dispose of the nuclear waste before installing new materials.

The worst thing a husband can do is put his wife in shutdown mode—because at that point, he'll have to deal with some nuclear issues. Why? The woman no longer feels she can tell her husband the truth. She can't sit down with him and say, "This is how I feel." So she ends up becoming foolish and trusting somebody else. Emotionally, she starts plucking her house down…because she can't trust the one who's supposed to be building her *up*.

"Shut down" forces a man to think about what he needs to do to bring this nuclear reactor back up to profit—because when his wife is no longer invested emotionally in the relationship, it's dangerous for him to be around her. At any moment, she could explode in his face. At this point, excuses won't do. Flowers and candy won't help. The only thing that can stop this explosion is *change*. If the man doesn't grow, it's over.

To be fair, he really doesn't intend for this to happen. Shut down is the result of poor communication, whether about a present or future event. As a result, the relationship isn't quarantined; it's not clarified; it hasn't been prepared to deal with issues that could kill your relationship and take out everything that's closest to you.

Listen to me, brother. The best indicator of your intentions is *change* and *growth*. If you keep doing the same thing over and over, eventually your wife's going to shut down so low that she'll never hear you or trust you again.

A foolish woman tends to think she can justify her shut down by telling everybody about her pain. So she starts talking to other people to rationalize how emotionally detached she's become. And sister, this is where a wife begins to pluck things down with her hands. James 3:8–15 says,

> *But the tongue can no man tame; it is an unruly evil, full of deadly poison. Therewith bless we God, even the Father; and therewith curse we men, which are made after the similitude of God. Out of the same mouth proceedeth blessing and cursing. My brethren, these things ought not so to be. Doth a fountain send*

forth at the same place sweet water and bitter? Can the fig tree, my brethren, bear olive berries? either a vine, figs? so can no fountain both yield salt water and fresh. Who is a wise man and endued with knowledge among you? let him shew out of a good conversation his works with meekness of wisdom. But if ye have bitter envying and strife in your hearts, glory not, and lie not against the truth. This wisdom descendeth not from above, but is earthly, sensual, devilish.

You cancel your own anointing when you curse what God has blessed. Resist the devil when he entices you to become negative in your relationship. Don't call your best friend and complain about your husband's shortcomings. Take your cares to the Lord. He'll cover you and give you sound wisdom to build your house.

But the wisdom that is from above is first pure, then peaceable, gentle, and easy to be intreated, full of mercy and good fruits, without partiality, and without hypocrisy. And the fruit of righteousness is sown in peace of them that make peace (James 3:17–18).

So, sister, don't hurt a brother by plucking down your relationship. Help him by learning how to tell him the truth in love. Sow peace into your marriage. Let God give you wisdom, and above all, develop the habit of being totally honest with your husband.

Don't let him think that simply working, bringing home a paycheck, and paying a couple of bills are enough for you. Don't hurt him by being quiet and emotionally withdrawn, *when God created you to give him savor.* You'll hurt your man if you don't learn to be honest about how you really feel and who you really are. Say to him, "I need you to know that in order for me to build our home, I need you to be in agreement with me. I need you to support me in this and hear my vision for the house. I need you to understand where I believe we can go if we can change how we do things."

Help your husband develop the ability to hear you by cultivating healthy communication. Otherwise, you'll hurt him, he'll hurt you, and your house won't be able to stand. Don't be foolish and emotional, giving the power of your hands over to somebody else—because when you start telling your cousin, sister, girlfriend, or co-worker about your relationship, it will immediately attack the credibility, integrity, and validity of your marriage.

Please understand, I'm not saying every man has an ear to hear his wife. Men are generally bull-headed and egotistical, "I'm the man, I've got it all together, I don't need your help…I was good without you." Men can say a whole lot of things that are mean, cruel, and ugly. When the rubber hits the road, though, a husband cannot make it ten minutes without a godly wife.

So, sister, do everything you can to avoid shutting down—because when shut down occurs, the only thing that will bring you back to him is hope. Please don't hurt a brother by holding in your pain. Come to the place where you can share honestly with him about where you are. That way, you can keep hope alive and continue building your house. Tell him, "If you do that one more time, this will happen inside of me… I need you to be very careful, as I don't know if I'll be able to recover and be the same woman you love right now."

Let Wisdom Build Your House

I realize a woman loves her husband so much that she wants to give him nine lives. *Consider this: maybe he only needs three.* Be honest with him, for when you tell the truth, you'll be healing yourself *and* protecting your house. Trying to hide your pain to avoid hurting his feelings isn't healthy. Hurt his feelings. Let him cry for a while. He'll get over it. Recovery can be a painful process. Your husband might have to take a long walk, but he'll love you for telling him the truth.

Real love isn't telling your husband what's convenient for him. It's telling him what's going to make your lives better. It's learning to be skillful and strategic about building your house. Tell him, "This discussion isn't about me; it's about us." In this context, you won't be *arguing* with him; you'll be *strengthening* your relationship. If you want the best for your home, you'll be sensitive about how you approach your husband because what you say to him also affects you. Be wise...build your house by using words that will cause your relationship to grow.

Pain is the result of wisdom being ignored—so it's actually pointing you to God. *Build*...don't pluck down. God is letting certain issues come to the surface so that you can deal with them and become stronger. Embrace every challenge as an opportunity to grow, and celebrate what God has given you. Use the anointing God has placed on *your* hands *to build*.

CHAPTER 8

I'm Not Your Momma

**A foolish son is the calamity of his father:
and the contentions of a wife are a continual dropping.
Proverbs 19:13**

If anyone understood women, it was probably King Solomon...he had a few hundred wives. Personally, I don't understand how he developed the capacity to be a husband to so many women. I've been blessed with one, virtuous wife...and she keeps me on my toes!

To be honest, I think it would be harder for a man to deal with one wife than for one woman to deal with a few hundred husbands. It's really the flip of the script. And I'm not referring to anything sensual. I'm talking about personality and responsibility. If you don't agree, start by considering this: *A man can't take care of four children, but a woman can.* How is she able to take care of four sons and a husband? Try giving a man four daughters and a wife (to care for in the same way)...it would be amazing if he could handle it.

A woman is made to nurture a variety of relationships in the home. On the other hand, a man can love his wife and children, but will he nurture them? A wife's anointing to nurture is a powerful blessing in the home, but it can lead to problems if her husband hasn't let go of the past. Let's look at Proverbs 19:13 from the Amplified Bible:

> *A self-confident and foolish son is the [multiplied] calamity of his father, and the contentions of a wife are like a continual dripping [of water through a chink in the roof].*

Many teach this scripture from the wrong perspective. They claim the woman is wrong because *she has issues*. If so, we must ask, *why does she have issues?* Does she stir herself up and become contentious without cause? I believe her contention is related to her husband's foolishness (and notice he's referred to as a "son")—because men generally don't understand and respect the gift a woman is to their life. And this misunderstanding traces all the way back to their roots.

In the dictionary, *contention* is very close to *content*. The words appear to be very similar—they even sound almost the same—but the meanings are totally opposite. The first means *struggle, strife,* and *conflict*; the second means to be *satisfied*.[1] *The revelation is this*: A man who is satisfied with *what used to be* will have constant conflict with his wife.

Something else is significant. In the Hebrew, a *continual dropping* (KJV) comes from two root words. The first means "...to follow close," and the second "...to weep" (Strong's, #H2956; #H1812/#H1811). Brother, when you treat your wife like your mother (in the sense that she must nurture you like a son), you'll break her heart. And when you expect her to settle for yesterday's best, tears will follow closely. Contention will be in your home. If you fail to see your wife's potential or to receive her healing in your life—you're definitely going to have problems. Jesus said,

> *For this cause shall a man leave his father and mother, and cleave to his wife; and they twain shall be one flesh: so then they are no more twain, but one flesh. What therefore God hath joined together, let not man put asunder* (Mark 10:7–9).

Notice the revelation. Jesus didn't say the woman had to leave *her* parents—because she loves automatically. She gives everything she is and cleaves to her husband. A man, however, likes things the way they always were. He may not realize that he's trying to go back to yesterday—*he's just being consistent.* Hear me, brother; when you sense tension in your home and your wife's tears are dropping continually, *contention is there.*

Ask yourself, *why is she being contentious?* Then look in the mirror. A contentious woman is living in a constant state of conflict and struggle. She's being prodded in her emotions because there's opposition to what she needs to *become.* Listen to wisdom. Stop trying to make your wife into somebody she's not.

It wounds a woman when she's serving breakfast and her husband says, "*My mother* made biscuits *like this...*" Infuriated, she spits back at him, "Well, I'm not your momma!" She's trying to build her house, and he's still *back at home* with the first woman he ever loved. *Contention.* Boys have a natural love for their mothers, and that's wonderful—but when a boy becomes a man, he must let go of childish things (1 Corinthians 13:11).

And sister, remember…this is why you must never call for a boy in your relationship. It could ultimately bring a lot of tears in your life. If you do, you can become the kind of wife who puts her husband on the roof (I'll get more into this later).

Let's move on. A real problem occurs when a man begins to identify something about his wife that reminds him of his mother. It might be her eyes. It could be the way she walks. It might be the way she talks, or her smile, or her hair…or even the way she cooks (or maybe doesn't cook). Then a spiritual attachment to his boyhood can form and be difficult to break.

As a woman, there's a maternal gift in you that naturally relates to your mother-in-law. And it's basically good when a man finds some similarities (hopefully he loves his mother so much that he'll treat you right and adore you), but it can become contentious when he tries to get the same thing from you that he used to get from his mother. This isn't reality.

For example, my mom is a great cook. She cooks whenever my father's in town, or at least five times a week. When I was growing up, my parents had a Sunday morning tradition. He'd get up, eat his beef bacon and toast, enjoy a cup of tea, and head off to church. (It's hard to preach on an empty stomach.) Some mornings, if he wanted a bit more and really felt like he was going to preach hard that day, my mother would make grits for him. And her grits would make you want to slap an elephant!

Whenever I call their home and my father happens to be eating, *I can smell the aroma all the way from Delaware to Washington, D.C.* I can just see the rye bread, toasted and buttered… I can see the steam rising up from the teacup, with lemon juice on the side; I can visualize the plate that's been warmed up with care…and I can even see the silverware. In my mind, I can almost touch the chair that used to be half turned, waiting for me to sit down.

Before I married Juanita, I used to get a little jealous on Sunday mornings. So I created a tradition of my own. I'd get up early that morning, go to a favorite restaurant, and enjoy a nice breakfast. Then I'd be off to church. This became my Sunday routine, for I knew what it could do for me in the pulpit.

I don't try to make Juanita my "momma." If I did, I'd have a contentious woman on my hands. I love my wife, so I allow her to be who she is. Seriously, though, there's a side of her that's so much like my mother. To start, my mother is from New York, so she's a New Yorker at heart. If you mess with her, she'll cut your throat, bury you, and tell Jesus you died (figuratively speaking, of course). My mother's *straight up* like that. She definitely doesn't pull any punches. I think that's why she and Juanita get along so well; they're both *straight-up* people.

I can't deal with a woman who doesn't tell me the truth, and being candid is one of Juanita's greatest strengths. I couldn't be happier…because I can't take a woman who's timid. Not too long ago, I was picking up Juanita from the airport and preparing to take her bags to the car when she reached over and said, "Let me help you." I said, "No, I've got it." She said, "No, let me help you…" My wife is super strong. It isn't obvious when looking at her, but she can carry some weight.

Anyway, she said to me, "I'm going to grab this…*and* that…" and it was done. I couldn't help saying, "That's what I like about you. You can throw that bag around. You can easily carry it by yourself." My wife is definitely not a weakling.

This is one of the areas where she and my mother differ. You wouldn't catch my mother lifting weights. She'd look you in the eyes and say, *straight up*, "Baby, if I have to lose weight, I'm going to lose it *my way*." So while my wife and mother do share some commonalities, they're uniquely different.

Confronting the Nature of a Woman

Let's go back to Proverbs 19:13.

...and the contentions of a wife are a continual dropping.

Let me explore another revelational truth: *A woman doesn't like to drop anything*. In fact, it's against her nature. She naturally protects and nurtures what belongs to her. This is why she packs a carton of eggs differently than a man—because all the while, she's thinking how they'll crack if she puts them in the car the wrong way. A man, on the other hand, would turn the egg carton to the side and cram it into the trunk of the car. "Oh, no, no, no…" she'd object, "that's the egg bag." She has twelve bags, and she remembers which one contains the eggs! A woman never wants anything to crack, drop, or be broken.

So when she drops something, it's painful, because her whole life is about *protecting*—her child, lifestyle, love, hopes, dreams, and desires. When something drops from a woman's life, *it hurts*. And when it happens *continually*, it becomes unbearable.

Let's go to Proverbs 27:15.

A continual dropping in a very rainy day and a contentious woman are alike.

When she's suffering from a contentious spirit, a woman starts dropping signals of aggravation, discomfort, frustration, and (husband, you're not going to like this one) hatred. She loves you, but she'll start hating you when you refuse to hear her.

Watch out when a woman starts dropping things—because a storm is coming. No matter how big the umbrella, you're still going to get drenched. The Amplified Bible calls it, *"...a day of violent showers...."* Have you ever been in a violent rainstorm and tried to put up an umbrella? You still get wet down to your toes because the wind is picking up sheets of rain and slapping you in the face.

You almost have to double-dare yourself to go outside... and you wouldn't even think about it unless it was an absolute emergency. So you run out, trying to beat the waves of pounding water, and you're getting beat up: whether you turn, duck, try to cover your head, or even run backwards. The storm is that violent.

When it rains, it pours. One of the worst things that could happen for a man is to be in a room with a contentious woman—because she's going to multiply all the heartaches he's given her and slam them right in his face. She'll lock the door, stand in front of it, and give him a piece of her mind before she storms out. Oh, yes! When a woman gets contentious, she'll demand, "We need to talk *right now*. I mean RIGHT NOW." Brother, if you're not at home, you'll be coming home soon. You'll stop whatever you're doing and make your way to see her, for she's not angry—*she's contentious*. She's ready to butt heads with you. And it's most likely about something you keep doing that's been rubbing her the wrong way for too long.

Notice that verse 15 in the Amplified Bible marries a *"contentious woman"* with *"violent showers."* So you can just imagine how this scenario builds. Consider how a rainy day develops. Some days are beautiful, with no clouds and a wonderful temperature; but when certain things in the atmosphere collide, moisture begins to rise and it starts collecting in the air. Then finally, the downpour begins.

The question is, is there contention in the clouds for you? Let me tell you how to know for sure. *Whatever a man gives to a woman, she multiplies it and gives it right back.* So, brother, if you don't like contention, change what you're giving her.

A wife defines the problems in the relationship, and it usually comes out in the form of a disagreement. This happens because she hasn't been able to share with you how she really feels about a certain situation. And if truth be told, you haven't been sensitive to her needs. The tension keeps building in her day by day. You, on the other hand, don't have a clue about what she's struggling with, so finally she explodes—and then you have to deal with it.

The fact is, you're stuck in something *old* while she's expecting something *new*. You've become redundant in an area because you're used to being consistent. She wants something new, fresh, and different. She makes a gesture to introduce you to change, but you just don't get it. And the struggle continues. The problem is, you've forgotten the situation and moved back into your routine. This inattention keeps nagging at her until she comes to you in a storm.

For example, let's say your wife told you last year that she didn't like Dairy Queen. "Can we please go to Ben and Jerry's?" she asked. You conceded. The next time, because

Dairy Queen is so close and Ben and Jerry's is ten more miles down the road, you just wanted to swing by DQ. Your budget is set for that; your taste is set...*you still haven't grown to the level of Ben and Jerry's*. So every time your wife wants ice cream, you default to Dairy Queen.

The truth is, *you're comfortable there*. She prefers Ben and Jerry's for good reason. She discovered the ice cream while shopping one day and fell in love with it. Now, she wants to keep sharing this new experience with you. And the whole time she was planning to pay for it—but you're stuck on your old favorite. So you close yourself to experiencing something better with the woman you love.

She's simply saying, "Trust me. If you get used to driving the extra ten minutes, you'll never go back to Dairy Queen." Then contention comes when you start telling her, "I grew up on Dairy Queen." And she's thinking, *Well...now it's time to grow up on Ben and Jerry's*. It hurts a woman when she has to drop her growth to be stuck someplace where there are only three flavors. She's trying to expand your horizons.

Another good example is what happens when a woman chooses where she'd like to go on vacation. She says, "Oh honey, look...this would be a great place." The man says, "Oh no, we're going back to Disney." She can't believe it. "We've been to Disneyland *ten times*. Can't we try Hawaii, or somewhere in the Islands...maybe St. Thomas, or Barbados? It only costs $300 for three days." She's got a good point, but he says, "I know baby, *but no*." He's stuck on the rides. She's grown up, but he still wants to jump on the roller coaster. He still wants to drive the bumper cars. In short, he's stuck being momma's little boy.

Truthfully, part of a wife's role is to experience the *old thing* with her man. However, a woman gets tired of redundancy without growth. So this wife keeps making suggestions about a great vacation, and he keeps shooting them down. And what really amazes her is he's willing to spend $700 to go somewhere he's already been ten times over. *He could save $400 and try something new.* Still, he wants to go back to enjoy the rides…and she's tired of going to a theme park. She's thinking, *How many times do you want to hug Goofy?*

Simple things like this can bring contention in your relationship, for when a woman feels like she's being ignored, *it reveals a problem.* The man is still stuck on what was good enough for his momma and family. *He hasn't tapped into who his wife is or who she desires to become.* Contention definitely rises when a man expects his wife to do things the way his mother always did.

I know this is a little heavy—but subconsciously, it's real. These are the things couples don't generally talk about, but they definitely impact the relationship. So, brother, scrape it up and start dealing with it. Honestly, your wife simply wants to be acknowledged—and the new things she keeps suggesting to you *aren't just about her.* She's trying to build her house. God created her to seek out new and better things for your family.

How I Avoided Contention

I faced an interesting dilemma around the time of the Iraqi conflict. My wife had told me she'd never been to Paris, so I said, "No problem. I'll take you there." Then the war began, and all the political developments hit the news daily. So I started having second thoughts. Knowing the tension between

France and the United States, I also wasn't sure if we'd have more problems going through French Customs, being Americans. In the meantime, Juanita was doing a beautiful job planning the wedding celebration. Her theme was "Paris in the Springtime," so I had a little incentive to make her dream happen. I needed God's wisdom.

I was really praying about it, so I started making alternative plans to go to Hawaii (I've never been there, and neither has Juanita.) We were almost settled on these plans when I realized they'd never really "clicked" in my spirit.

Then I had to fly to London, and I sat next to a man who was working hard the majority of the flight. We didn't talk until afterwards, while walking through the gate at the airport. I said something to him like, "Isn't it amazing what's happening in France?" He turned and said, "Yeah, I have a French boss who works in America..." He finished talking and we went our separate ways.

After I arrived at the hotel, my wife and I were talking about our honeymoon and I said, "I really feel in my spirit that I still need to take you to Paris. I already have the tickets, and I've already found the perfect hotel. It's just something I feel I need to do."

Not long after that I was in Washington, D.C., driving and talking to her on my way home. She was in Chicago handling some things for the wedding. I missed her so badly, I went to Papa Johns and got a nice pizza to eat all by myself. As we were talking, she reminded me, "The very first time we met, it wasn't even a date. It was at a meeting in Chicago...so we need to end up in Chicago." I liked the idea, and interestingly, I'd already been thinking about it and was already considering having another minister preach at our church, which would give us a few more days for our honeymoon.

Then I made the decision, "This is my honeymoon celebration, and I'm going to take another Tuesday night to enjoy it." So I told Juanita, "Honey, I feel that. You know what? When we come back to the States, let's fly to Chicago, hang out at the water tower, and just enjoy each other." "That's good," she responded, "because it allows us to come full circle."

I arrived at home carrying the leftover pizza and sat down to begin dealing with some pastoral issues. Then it came to me how ministry used to keep me on edge. No matter where I was or what was happening, I always sensed an urgency to get back for church. That's when I had a revelation. Over the years, Juanita had given so much for ministry that I didn't want her to drop her desires for our honeymoon. If I cut our special time short, ministry could ultimately become a storm of contention in our marriage. I didn't want that. And more important than anything else—*it was her season of celebration.*

What Kind of Man Are You?

I try hard not to live in the past or to impose my mother's behavior on my wife. While my mother is amazing and is perfect for my father, I realize *I'm not my father.* In most cases where there's an identity problem in a marriage, *the man is trying too hard to be his daddy.* And when a man tries to be his father, he automatically imposes the same type of behavior on his wife. Then contention hits because she's crying out, "I didn't marry your father. *I married you*…so don't try to be your dad—*because I'm not your momma!*"

Sister, it's important that you learn to discern the differences between your husband and his father. This way, you can identify if things start to get strained around your house and get the wisdom of God to deal with it.

I have somewhat of a problem because people tell me I look a lot like my father. Many times they expect me to be just like him. If the truth be told, I really do have a lot of his mannerisms, but there are some ways I'm absolutely different. And it's all good. I recognize my differences have allowed me to venture out and try new things that fit my lifestyle.

If you're a carbon copy of your parents, you'll only be as great as they've become. On the other hand, if you have their DNA along with (the potential of) your own, matured personality, you can become greater than your parents are—because now *you've stepped into your destiny.*

Have you ever known somebody who grew up in the country and then moved to the city? Usually it's difficult for that person to adapt to living in an urban environment. This is what happens in a contentious relationship. A husband is so much a copy of his early environment that he finds it extremely difficult to become something new in another setting. His personality doesn't want to adapt.

Let's return to Proverbs 19:13.

> **A foolish son is the calamity of his father:** *and the contentions of a wife are a continual dropping* (emphasis mine).

A father is responsible for training a son to become wise—that's why it's a tragedy when the opposite happens. In reality, *calamity* occurs when a father *breathes wickedness* into his son's life (Strong's #H1942/#H1933). And the wickedness is this: He's acting in a way that's the exact opposite of what God intended. Sadly, the son follows suit.

This can present another dilemma. When a woman has to train her son, he's more than likely going to grow up *timid*, *weak*, and *feminine*. Think about it. Have you ever known a man who's always smacking his lips or popping chewing gum in his mouth like a girl? He got it from his momma. No offense intended, but if a son isn't birthed from a true, spiritual father, he can become a fool, *especially* if God doesn't intervene in his life.

A mother cannot become a father, no matter how much she tries. Please understand, I'm not saying a woman can't do a good job as a single parent. I'm simply saying that it's difficult to be both a nurturer *and* a father figure. Sister, if you're raising a son alone, try to find an uncle or cousin you can trust to mentor him. Find a man who will teach him how to fish, shovel snow, change a tire on a bike, and other such things. In short, he needs to be taught *manhood*. If your son isn't taught to be a man, then he could try to take what he loves most *in you* and project it onto his wife.

A son brings calamity to a father who doesn't teach him the wisdom of God. This could mean dad is in the home and not involved, or dad is not in the home at all. Many men seem to think *giving things* to their sons is most important. I disagree. Although a father should take pride in providing for his family, *the greatest thing he can impart is truth*. So if he's wise, he'll tell his son, "You may look like me, but God created you to be your own man. As you seek Him, He'll bless your life in ways you never imagined."

How Healing Comes

On one occasion while Juanita was in London, we had a major blowup. I mean, we had a real disagreement. The kind where you're yelling into the phone while pulling it away from your ear. You know, the type of disagreement where you hang up on the other person four times. *It was one of those.* And it wasn't like we could fly two hours and resolve the issue face-to-face; traveling to London takes nine hours. So later, when the opportunity came for me to actually *be with her* in London, I promised myself I'd make it special.

On Saturday night, after finishing her *Women on the Front Line* meeting, she said, "Honey, go buy a leather jacket." I said, "A leather jacket—*no problem.*" So I went out, purchased a leather jacket, and bought a blue shirt to go with my jeans. She looked beautiful, and I was looking pretty nice myself. We rode through London, then stopped at a nice French restaurant in Soho. There we picked a quiet corner and started looking at the menu.

We had no idea what we were ordering! The entire menu was in French, so we tried to find any words that looked like *chicken, duck,* or anything English. While we were sitting and talking, it came to my spirit what was really happening. If I had rushed back for church (instead of spending quality time on this trip with my wife), *I would have never healed the place of our contention.*

So, brother, wherever your wife has been wounded, take her back there and start over again. Start fresh *in that place.* Do something you've never done before, and you'll break the spirit of contention.

In the end, our first blowout (when Juanita was in London) actually turned out to be a tremendous blessing. Let me explain. Disagreements are healthy as long as you can get to the other side and grow. That's what happened when I remembered the conflict and decided to stay longer with my wife in London. The ultimate goal is to heal contentious places. If you keep this in mind, that storm won't blow your way again.

A good disagreement will make you change so the issue doesn't come back to the surface. So if you're constantly disagreeing about the same thing—or, sister, if you continue to battle with the same emotions—the disagreement wasn't productive. On the other hand, if you disagree about something and heal the issue, the next disagreement won't have anything to do with it. *That's a good disagreement*, for you emerged having birthed something new in your relationship.

The truth is, a woman disagrees because she wants to correct a situation. She really wants to get it right. For example, I'm an Ivy League kind of guy. I used to wear white turtlenecks with sweaters all the time. One day, Juanita looked at me and said, "I don't like the turtleneck." "It's *me*," I protested. I had a real problem with her criticism, even though she meant it to be constructive. "I have five white turtlenecks, and they fit me just fine; I know how to crunch them up and position them just right…*look at me!* I like them exactly the way they are…why are you messing with my Ivy League stuff?" I started walking around, stomping hard, copping an attitude.

Then she said, "Would you mind trying a black turtleneck?" *I tried it, and she was right.* At that moment, I had a choice. I could either let a white turtleneck bring a storm of contention (because mothers always affirm their sons when it comes to dressing), or heed the wise counsel of my wife. I decided to confess, "Honey, you're right. It does look better." Juanita's a very visual, graphically oriented person. She's *par excellence* when it comes to colors and concepts.

Brother, when your wife's trying to upgrade you from a son to a husband, you may resist change in an effort to stay with what makes you feel comfortable. *Watch out*...your momma's personality could be keeping you from adapting to something new. Interestingly, I don't wear white turtlenecks anymore. Now I recognize white is too bland for a colorful person like me. My wife helped me to understand this. I look better in caramel brown, black, or maybe a soft purple. They accentuate my features better than white.

We have to be honest with ourselves. Our egos always say, "I'm right." Yet, a woman will come along and challenge it, saying, "*This is better*, honey. You might be right, but if you'd just try what I'm suggesting, I think you'll like it a lot better."

On the other hand, if I tell Juanita, "Baby, you sure look good in those jeans." She'll say, "Let's stop for a minute at this store...um hum... Does this fit? Does this look good to you, honey?" "Yeah, hold on to those. Get about five more pairs." Juanita buys what I like seeing her in. So while we're walking around, I'm holding onto the back of her jeans. I'm being a good husband; I'm making sure she's not going anywhere! And she does the same with me.

So get rid of contention. You don't need it! It's a signal that communication needs to happen on a certain, sensitive issue. And obviously, God wants you to deal with it so your marriage can grow. Work through it, and make sure to celebrate change by doing the *little things*.

This brings me back to my five white turtlenecks. I decided to put them out where Juanita could see them, and then say, "Honey, can you throw these away?" I'm going to celebrate the change she brought in me.

As God gives me the capacity, I'm going to nurture our relationship. I couldn't be more aware that my wife is not my momma—she's a priceless gift to my life that I intend to cherish.

A little change won't hurt me. In fact, it will bring great rewards. *Absolutely.*

Endnote

1. Steinmetz, *Webster's Dictionary*, 208.

CHAPTER 9

Brother, Don't Be Crazy

**It is better to dwell in a corner of the housetop,
than with a brawling woman in a wide house.
Proverbs 21:9**

In most species, the female has the strongest killer instinct. It's built into her nature so that she can create a safe place to nurture and develop her offspring. When a threat arises, she extinguishes it. She'll attack anything that comes too close, and then she'll chase it so far away that it won't ever come back. In some species, the mate will return and try to kill the young...and if that happens, she'll turn and fight him just like she would any other predator.

Animals can't rationalize their behavior; they simply act on instinct. Humans, however, are distinct. When we choose to submit to God, everything lines up accordingly. When we don't, everything falls out of balance. Although man was created far superior to animals, we can't evade certain laws of the universe.

For example, according to Hebrew thought, the aspect of *man* and *woman* that reflects the image of God is derived from a word that means *fire*. This fire made Adam and Eve unique above all other beings. It gave them the ability to achieve dominion, attain wisdom, and develop culture. On the other hand, if it wasn't controlled and directed by the Lord, the same fire would cause destruction.

This principle carries over into marriage. If a man and woman have God in the midst of their relationship, the union will be godly. If not, it becomes destructive—harming their relationship and threatening everything around them.[1]

Let's go one step further from a Hebrew commentary:

> If the man is worthy, the woman will be a helper. If he is unworthy, she will be against him. The ideal marriage is not necessarily one of total agreement. Often, it's the woman's responsibility to oppose her husband and prevent him from acting rashly, or to help him achieve a common cause by questioning, criticizing, and discussing.[2]

First, let me clarify. This doesn't mean a wife shouldn't submit. It means she has a specific anointing and purpose to help her husband stay in position to receive from the Lord. If he removes himself from God's covering, he automatically uncovers her. Then she has to go to war against spiritual forces that are trying to destroy the home.

Let's go to Proverbs 21:9:

> *It is better to dwell in a corner of the housetop, than with a brawling woman in a wide house.*

The true meaning of this text has to start with the word *brawling*. Brawling is a very pain-filled word. It's actually drawn from the same root as *contention*, but it differs in intensity (Strong's, #H4079/#H4066/#H1777). Contention is like a dripping, or a violent rain. Brawling is "a noisy fight or quarrel, esp. in a public place…a bubbling or roaring noise, as water flowing over a rocky bed."[3] Brawling takes contention to a new level.

Remember, an argument can be productive as long as you get to the other side of it and change. When a couple argues, they disagree over different points of view. They simply see things differently, so they work it out and come to a common ground. Arguments escalate to a brawling state when a person feels violated. Someone has become offended. A principle has been broken. A trust has been shattered. This brings us back to honesty—because as long as you trust your spouse, you can come to a solution. When trust is gone, brawling begins.

Bear with me, brother, because I'm about to touch on a sensitive issue. Too often, men mislead their wives with broken promises. It's a boyish way of manipulating a woman to appease her so you don't have to change. The problem is, your mistruth is usually discovered later. Even if you think the matter is insignificant, every lie shreds the fibers of your relationship. And one day, your wife will kick into a brawling mode—because deception is the child of Satan, *and she's anointed to bruise his head.*

It's one thing to misunderstand a matter and argue. It's entirely another when miscommunication and misuse are intentional. Brother, when you deceive your wife with empty promises, you're destroying your own home. Colossians 3:9–10 says,

> *Lie not one to another, seeing that ye have put off the old man with his deeds; and have put on the new*

*man, which is renewed in knowledge after the image
of him that created him.*

If you act like the devil and dishonor the truth, she'll lose respect for you...and you may never win it back. Women respect honesty. For example, a wife will bear with her unsaved husband who's honest about who he is and how he deals with her. However, if her husband is saved and dishonest—*fire is unleashed.* Her survival instinct kicks in, and she'll absolutely take him down because he's threatening the stability of her house.

Yes, the same woman who beats down the enemy on your behalf will turn and come after you when her emotional temperature bubbles over the boiling point. Uncovering her through deception unleashes a wildfire in her emotions. And this is when she reverts to her "guttural" instincts.

Here's a revelation. For the woman, escalating to a brawling state is a long, painful process—because Eve was the mother of all living things (see Genesis 3:20). When a woman sees "Adam" (i.e., her husband) destroying their lives through deception, she starts "plucking" fruits from the tree in an attempt to preserve them: love, joy, peace, patience, kindness, goodness, faithfulness, gentleness...*and then finally*, self control (Galatians 5:22–23). *Then the firestorm begins.* Remember, a woman doesn't like anything to drop, so every time good fruit falls to the ground, it stabs at her nature. To her, this goes beyond aggravation, for the principle of life has been broken. Then she escalates into a state of warfare.

The Danger of Broken Promises

By the time she reaches the brawling stage, a woman's pain is unimaginable. So if a man is truly honest, he'll say to himself, "I saw it coming"—*because she doesn't just click into a brawling mode.* She doesn't just wake up one morning and say, "I'm going to brawl today." When a husband compromises the integrity of God's Word and makes a promise he doesn't intend to keep, ultimately, he's going to have a battle. And worse yet, he's canceling his own anointing as the head of his household.

Here's an example. Let's say you promised your wife a nice, week-long vacation in San Diego. Unfortunately, things weren't working out as planned—but instead of being honest with her, you string her along with empty promises. Then the day before you're supposed to leave (after she's prepared everything for the trip), you spring the bad news. And because you know that you've been wrong, you're in a self-protective mode.

Understandably, she's upset and confronts you, "You promised me that we were going to go to San Diego for vacation, and now we can go out of town for only two days instead of a week." Feeling guilty, you hide behind your ego and justify your deception. You won't admit something went wrong, and you were either too lazy to take care of it or it was beyond your control. Be honest with yourself *and* your wife. How can you justify building her expectations, letting her go through the whole, disappointing process, without telling her the truth? A child hides things when they don't pan out.

Brother, don't be crazy. Situations like this will ultimately tear your relationship apart. The wounds of broken trust cannot heal overnight—because it takes a process for your wife to escalate into brawling.

What Happened to Knowledge?

Now, sister, just to be fair, every man has made a promise he wasn't able to keep. And deception isn't always the culprit. Remember, a man must see a need before he'll adapt to meet it. So sometimes it takes a process of him giving his word and not keeping it to break this pattern of behavior. He loves you, but he may not understand your attention and sensitivity to his words.

This takes me back to 1 Peter 3:7:

Likewise, ye husbands, dwell with them according to knowledge, giving honour unto the wife, as unto the weaker vessel, and as being heirs together of the grace of life; that your prayers be not hindered.

On the other hand, brother, if you've been dwelling with your wife *according to knowledge*, you should have known better. You're supposed to understand her emotional environments: her needs, likes, dislikes, hopes, and dreams. In short, you know what makes her tick. You understand her emotions. Dealing with knowledge means you make the effort to make things right for her. You sacrifice *your desire* to provide what she wants and needs.

Don't be silly enough to think you can tantalize her with a promise, and then break it without facing the repercussions. Don't play with your wife like that. Be a *straight-up* man—because more than anything, a woman hates for a man to know her emotions and play them. Let's go back to Proverbs 21:9:

It is better to dwell in a corner of the housetop, than with a brawling woman in a wide house.

I want to bring clarity to the term, *wide house*. The word *wide* comes from a Hebrew root that means to charm, or fascinate by casting a spell (Strong's, #H2267/#H2266). Here's the revelation. When you try to fascinate your wife by making promises to appease her, you're living in a *wide house*. God's not going to honor a lie, and before long, she's going to put you on the roof.

Women aren't stupid. They pick up pretty quickly when a man is trying to play their emotions by making false promises. They can sense when he's trying to *appease* a situation without *changing* to correct it. Hear me, brother. Ultimately, a man must take responsibility for his actions. So be wise and *knowledgeable* with your wife. Learn to confess, "I blew it. I was wrong." Be honest with yourself and your spouse. Don't try to evade responsibility by making excuses.

This ties back into being your own man. If your father was irresponsible, you don't have to be like him. Chances are you've already used this excuse with your wife. And believe me, it only works once. "Well, uh…when my father got paid, he carried all of his money in his pocket. He paid for things when he wanted to, and when he couldn't…he just stopped. So that's why I pay the bills this way. It's what I learned…."

Remember, a woman is committed to *change* and *growth*, so she'll never be satisfied with hearing the same excuses time and time again. So once you've dealt with a matter and corrected it, don't be crazy and do the same thing next week. Your wife will see the pattern, and you'll be headed for trouble. Stop playing the blame game. She'll pick up on it and remind you of the truth—*you should have been changing all along.*

When a man keeps breaking his promises, he's very self-ish. He doesn't care how it affects his wife, as long as it doesn't affect him. That's why God commanded the man to sacrifice himself for the woman. Brother, we're ultimately responsible to be unselfish so our families can be sanctified, cleansed, and ready for Christ's return (Ephesians 5:25–30). *So remember: Empty promises cancel your anointing—but if you build your wife, she'll build the house and make it your home.*

Can You Handle the Truth?

When a woman is brawling, she's reached the point of *blessing you out*, *throwing you out*, or *taking you out* altogether—because her spirit is warring against the enemy *she sees in you*. If you tried to ask, "What's making you so mad?" the truth would be like fiery charcoal smoldering in a pit. Her pain is so intense, it can turn you into white ash that crumbles at the slightest touch. *The truth is, when a woman brawls, she's dangerously past the point of working things out peaceably.*

The problem comes when a husband moves in *pride* instead of *knowledge*. Let me explain. When a man moves in pride, he's coddling his own weaknesses. When he moves in knowledge, he's embracing hers. As a godly man, you must embrace her weaknesses and minister to her needs as being special among women. Unfortunately, as soon as an argument flares up, men usually start to reminisce about the *good old days*—when he didn't have to be accountable in a relationship. So he pops off and says something stupid like, "Well, in my last relationship, I didn't have to…" "Who's the last relationship?" she cuts in. "You know…Sarah." *He's in trouble.* "Look," she snaps, "I'm not Sarah." Then the argument escalates.

The next thing you know, she's brawling. She starts telling him everything she hates about Sarah. "Sarah's bald-headed and ugly…and she's always wearing cheap weaves." *She's boiling hot.* He's not getting out of this until she shares her pain in full measure. At this point, the man is looking for the door and trying to plan out how quickly he can unlock it and escape. She senses it. So when he gets to the door, she adds, "And you'd better not go back to Sarah, either. If you do, I'm going to beat both of you down."

Let me tell you, brother, your wife isn't going to act saved all the time. So don't even say, "I thought you were saved" when she's brawling. She's sharp…she'll cut you down: "I am…*until you get on my nerves.*" Listen, brother, don't be crazy. Don't question your wife's salvation while she's brawling. The fact is, you're the reason for it. "Well, I thought you were saved," she'll say. "You're supposed to be the man of the house. Why aren't you keeping your word? You shout, dance, and act holy during church services—but you can't even make sure your family's taken care of."

A woman will take you down at the kneecap. And when she cuts you, *it's deep.* Don't expect her to offer you a Band-Aid, either; when she's brawling, she'll let you hobble for a while. You'll be on a stretcher before the battle is over.

Here's a paradox. When a man can't face and deal with his own issues, he can literally take everything down with him. Why? His earthly nature comes from Adam. So in the spirit realm, he's tied to the earth where all living things are planted. If he starts going under, everything else will follow. That's when a woman's emotional temperature goes beyond critical limits. Deep in her spirit, she's struggling against a dangerous, spiritual predator that's threatening her family's future.

Learn to Disarm a Brawling Spirit

It's better for you to develop the capacity to hear her out, and then say, "I'm going up to the roof. When you calm down, I'll be there. Just yell up from the window, call me on the cell, send me a text message, page me…*whatever.* Let me know when you've calmed down and are ready to talk." Brother, it can be a fatal mistake to think you can hold your own against a brawling woman. She's crouched down for the kill.

A woman will beat you down when she feels her rights have been violated. It's in her nature. So don't be surprised if you make her brawling come out and she attacks you. *Dwell with her according to knowledge*, especially since *your sin* probably caused this firestorm. She'll ultimately come back to her senses and say, "Oops! I forgot to tell you, I black out when I feel like somebody has betrayed me. I totally lose sense of what I'm doing…*I just react.* Ask my cousins, they know."

What can really be dangerous is when a woman used to be a tomboy—because while she was growing up, she probably became accustomed to punching boys. Let's look at a possible scenario. One day while she's hanging out with the boys, they all decide to go up into the tree house. The problem is, there are only six seats and seven children. So when she climbs up, she notices her seat has already been taken. She scans the room, finds the weakest boy, and then punches him out. "This is my seat," she demands.

This reveals another sensitive issue. A man should never hit a woman. When every part of her being is communicating wrath, the devil will tempt you to retaliate. Remember, you cannot become resentful. God has given you the *knowledge* to avoid becoming harsh, bitter, or destructive. If your wife literally loses it and starts swinging at you, simply *express* your strength. In other words, carefully restrain her and then say, "I'm not going to take this. You need to calm down."

In reality, however, it's still better for you to avoid physical contact and go up on the roof when a brawling woman has lost her sense of control. Let her release her pain, and then leave her alone until she's able to gain her composure. Don't tip the scales again. If you do, you may not live to see what's on the other side.

Brother, don't be crazy. You don't know how many men before you have broken promises in her life. So if you break your word, it only amplifies the previous lies. It's like she puts every new promise on top of a totem pole. All of the broken promises are showing her *negative, negative, negative*—and it's like a huge stick of dynamite. This is why *you* must keep *your promises*. Your word will become either the fuse that lights it or the cap that protects it from exploding. *Which will it be?*

My Brawling Experience

I used to have a super bad temper…and it traces back to when I was about three-and-a-half years old. Both of my parents were attending college. My father had just finished his Bachelor's degree and was in his Master's program, and my mother was working toward her undergraduate degree. They couldn't afford to take care of me while attending classes and working, so they sent me to stay with some good friends in

New York. They were great people, but because I wasn't a blood relative, I ran into some problems with their kids.

To make a long story short, we all went out to the playground one day (there were about nine of us). While we were playing, I decided that I wanted to jump on one of the monkey bars. *I didn't know it was Bobby Bill's bar.* Anyway, when he saw me, he jumped off of the swing and ran toward me screaming, "NO, NO, it's MINE..." and ripped me down off of the bar. The next thing I knew, they'd thrown me under the monkey bars and were kicking dirt all over me. To this day, I can still see their feet kicking around in the dirt.

That was when I discovered my bad temper. I remember it vividly. They were kicking like crazy...and then suddenly, it slowed down. I came out swinging. When I was finally able to make it through, my only thought was reaching the path that led to their apartment building...*then* if I could just make it to the elevator, I'd jump off on the third floor and run up six more steps to safety.

This affected my attitude toward people for years. It put me in a state of mind where I always thought somebody was trying to hurt me to get what he or she wanted. Every person represented a new head on the totem pole. So throughout my childhood, if somebody came after me or rejected me, my attitude was, "I'm going to kill you because I'm never going to let you get to the place where you can throw me under something I don't want to be under."

Brother, a woman doesn't want to be under (i.e., submitted to) a man who doesn't keep his promises. If you keep breaking your word, she'll eventually come out swinging...and she won't stop until she's extinguished the threat.

Let's go back briefly to my testimony. Even though I was saved, the issue was still there…*only suppressed*. I didn't realize how dysfunctional I'd become, since I'd locked the issue deep within my emotional past. Ultimately, I couldn't suppress it anymore, so I went through counseling. That's when I learned how to go back to the core of an issue. Through this process, I learned to document all the steps back to that experience on the playground. And I'm a better person today, now that I'm truthful with my emotions.

Brother, don't be crazy. Learn how to disarm a brawling woman. Use your God-given capacity to dwell with her *according to knowledge*. I've already touched on the fact that going to the roof is the first step in the disarming process. It allows her to calm down, and it prevents you from being tempted to retaliate. Let me balance this again by saying, *don't leave until God has provided a window*—otherwise, her emotions will remain uncovered and she'll think you don't care about how she feels. Listen until God releases you to your "corner" (Proverbs 21:9).

Secondly, make sure she knows how to locate you once she's calmed down. Don't go so far away that her spirit can't discern where you are. In other words, in her heart she's saying, "You can be on the rooftop because I'll know you're still close enough to protect me. Don't abandon your position, for I still need you to protect."

If you run out and leave her uncovered, you're in trouble. "Where were you?" she'll demand. "I went over to Sam's." "Why did you go over there?" Now you're really confused. You thought she needed some space—but you forgot to tell her exactly where you were going. You ran out of the house so quickly, you left your cell phone, and then you couldn't call back to check how she was doing.

That's the third step. Call her and say, "I'm over at Sam's house. I'm just going to watch a game, and I will be back in a couple of hours. If you need me, my cell phone is on. I'm here for you." In other words, *demonstrate you care, and healing will come.*

The truth is, you'll probably have to deal with her emotions for a while, for a brawling woman doesn't let you off the hook the next day. She'll make sure you remember, "You'd better not do it again." And she means it. She might even say, "If you do that again—that black frying pan in the kitchen is going to have your precious signature on it." Oh, yes! That pan will know you inside and out, for she'll personally assign it to your face if you mislead her again. Your dazed expression will be sitting on top of the burner, underneath the scrambled eggs.

She's thinking, *My emotions mean too much for you to keep ignoring them like some childhood game.* Listen to me, brother. Every promise you make to your wife is worth its weight in gold—*because she wants to believe in her lord.* You can't put a price tag on a truthful relationship. That's why Jesus said,

> *Heaven and earth shall pass away, but my words shall not pass away* (Matthew 24:35).

Think of it this way: It's probably a good sign that she brawled, for when you made her a promise, it really meant a lot. She trusted you to the extent that she exploded when you didn't come through. If she hadn't trusted you deeply, she wouldn't be angry at all. *Your wife honestly thought you'd perform your word*. This is what you need to focus on, and learn to celebrate, once you come down from the roof.

Lastly, when the firestorm is over, make sure you get to the root of the matter. By now, you should realize that denying the problem isn't going to help. Discuss, even document, where the problem began—even if you both have to trace it back to the beginning of your relationship. Identify the core issue that ignited the dynamite. Then repent and ask her forgiveness. Say, "I blew it; I'm wrong. You're right…help me to change." If you'll grow to this level of maturity, your relationship can be upgraded. And by bringing attention to a nagging issue, you'll disarm it in a positive way.

It's Time to Restore Your House

As a man, realize that certain circumstances can go beyond your control. So, brother, when something happens that could affect a promise you made to your wife, *be proactive.* Tell her as far in advance as possible, "You know, honey, there's a possibility this may not work out because..." Don't wait until the week of vacation to say, "We can't go." *Tell her the truth in love.* "Baby, our priorities have shifted. The plumbing needs to be repaired…" or, "The car really needs work, or we could end up stranded. Let me use part of the money I've been saving to handle this, and we can still take the kids on a two-day trip close by."

A woman rarely says *no* when a man is honest. Truth be told, she'd probably prefer to invest in something your family needs than to spend all of the money on pleasure.

Also keep in mind, *anytime you change, expect to be tested.* For example, I went to a meeting one day and took one of my deacons along. During this meeting, the person became highly disrespectful and insulted me. I told myself, "Tell yourself...*you're a Bishop*. Tell yourself...*you're a pastor*. Tell yourself...*you've been delivered*. Tell yourself *even though this person's kicking you out of the building like a thug to justify his own dysfunction, it won't cause you to become dysfunctional*." That situation definitely had the potential of turning into a brawl.

If the old me had shown up, there would have been serious problems—but the Holy Spirit grabbed me and said, "Keep your mouth shut and let him kick you out. Walk to you car, start it up, and keep going. Write a note of apology for anything you may have done wrong, for you have to become greater than everybody else's weaknesses. This is what qualified you."

Hear me, brother. You can't extinguish fire with fire. It will devour everything in its path. Remember Ephesians 5:25–30,

> *Husbands, love your wives, even as Christ also loved the church, and gave himself for it; that he might sanctify and cleanse it with the washing of water by the word, that he might present it to himself a glorious church, not having spot, or wrinkle, or any such thing; but that it should be holy and without blemish. So ought men to love their wives as their own bodies. He that loveth his wife loveth himself. For no man ever yet hated his own flesh; but nourisheth and cherisheth it, even as the Lord the church: for we are members of his body, of his flesh, and of his bones.*

Even if you've been wrong, you can still turn the situation around. Rise up in your anointing and embrace your wife for everything she is; *wash her pain away*. That's what qualifies you to be a husband.

Make it your goal to always be a man of your word. Don't make promises lightly, and keep them once you've made them. Recently, I noticed that whenever my wife asks me to promise her something, it's because she could trust the last time I kept my word. Believe me, it's a great thing when a woman says, "Promise me..." *It means she believes what you say is already done*. Brother, when your wife finds security in your word, she'll celebrate you and forget the pain of the past.

Endnotes

1. Rabbi Nosson Scherman, General Editor, *The Chumash*, The ArtScroll Series ®/Stone Edition (Brooklyn, New York, MESORAH PUBLICATIONS, Ltd., 1998, 2000), 13, "eish."

2. Ibid., 13.

3. Steinmetz, *Webster's Dictionary*, 117.

Chapter 10

Are You Willing to Listen to Love?

Finally, be ye all of one mind, having compassion one of another, love as brethren, be pitiful, be courteous: not rendering evil for evil, or railing for railing: but contrariwise blessing; knowing that ye are thereunto called, that ye should inherit a blessing.
1 Peter 3:8–9

It's interesting that God used a star to lead *wise men* to Jesus—and that a king tried to kill Him before He could reach maturity (Matthew 2:1–18). God sent this star for vision, direction, and inspiration; then He stirred up a king to threaten the eternal promise. Life is filled with paradoxes, and as you've learned, so is marriage. This is why wisdom is the principal thing (Proverbs 4:7). If your marriage is going to survive and fulfill the purposes of God, *wisdom must wash your life.* Everything requires a process.

A paradox is something that seems to contradict itself. This is usually the process of wisdom. So if you want to build a better marriage, you must start with God first. Otherwise, the enemy will try to eclipse your relationship and Light will fade away. To say it differently, spiritual life won't be flowing in your home.

God declared that marriage is honorable (Hebrew 13:4). It's a deep mystery that reflects Christ and the church (Ephesians 5:31–32). Then why are so many Christian marriages failing? Yes, true love is definitely a paradox.

The enemy goes about as a roaring lion, seeking whom he may devour (1 Peter 5:8). Yet, notice the word may implies he needs permission. *Here's the truth: Either you or your spouse has to give the devil permission to destroy your marriage.* Maybe you've been far away from God; maybe something from your childhood paralyzed your ability to love; maybe your intimacy needs a refreshing; or perhaps you just don't understand the opposite sex. My prayer is that you've become a person of "hearing." If so, you've begun the process of listening to love.

How Our Love Began

For our first date, I drove to New York and took Juanita to see a play in Manhattan. I had already picked out my clothes and everything else I thought I'd need for the trip. I had it timed down to the minute. When I checked into my hotel room, I started changing clothes and discovered the iron wasn't working. It took the hotel staff almost twenty minutes to bring a replacement—which ran me late picking her up. That really bothered me, since I'm a scheduled person. Finally, I arrived at her house with flowers in my hand, nicely wrapped in a box, and rang the doorbell.

As I mentioned before, her home is beautiful. I met a few of her friends, and then we left to enjoy our evening. After the play, we had a long discussion over dinner and took a taxi ride around the city...just talking. We took our time, learned a lot about each other—and found something that's real. I believe this is the reason we've been able to continue developing open, honest communication. And believe me, it's made all of the difference in our marriage.

Hear me, sister. Don't marry a man for what he has. Marry him for what he does for you. If your spirit comes alive when you're in his presence, he could be the man of your dreams. Take some time and let your spiritual relationship grow so that you'll be able to embrace him for who he really is. I came alive when I met Juanita. And the more time I spent with her, the more I knew that I'd gladly give my life for hers.

Juanita is the greatest wife in the world. To her, it didn't matter that she's one of the most celebrated international evangelists in the world today: She was ready and willing to celebrate coming into my life. I'll never forget when I first brought her to my place in Washington. I said to her, "Now let me explain something to you...I put a lot of emphasis into my work because that's where I am most of the time." She walked in, saw all of my computers and machines...and became a first-hand witness that I'm an information guerrilla. I said softly, "All right, just tell me the truth..." I'll never forget her response, "I know you're in the building stages of ministry and understand how you have to sacrifice. *You've already treated me how I need to be treated...*" She didn't see a bachelor pad; she sensed new life.

Always remember—what a person lacks, tells you what he or she needs. *So listen to love.* Instead of arguing or giving up, find out what your spouse doesn't have and cover that need. You see, Juanita didn't need another painting. She needed somebody to love her and to take her out—because she rarely did. She either traveled and ministered, or she stayed at home. Most men who wanted to date her tried to give her what she already had; I showed her I was ready to produce the things she had need of.

In return, I received a precious gift. I needed someone to love me and build her house into my home…and that's what I found in Juanita.

Learn to Find a Divine Balance

If you learn to meet each other's needs, you can you find true balance in your relationship. Let's go to Proverbs 16:11:

A just weight and balance are the LORD's: all the weights of the bag are his work.

This is a deep revelation. For a believer (and for everyone, for that matter), the Word of God determines a *just weight*. In other words, each partner should be fully committed to the marriage, but God determines how you should express your love. Keep it simple. Love God and learn to do what pleases your spouse. Then your marriage will remain intact.

The words, *weight* and *balance*, are based on the idea of "scales"—which speaks to your thought life (Strong's, #H6425/#H6424, #H3976/#H239). So as you each walk in the counsel of His Word, the "scales" of your relationship will start coming into balance.

Here's something powerful. The root word in Hebrew for *weights* means *to build* (Strong's, #H68/#H1129). So remember, God sees both husband and wife as builders in His kingdom. You simply build in different ways. Each of you has the ability to balance one another and affirm your love—the man leading and the woman following.

Let me share a great balancing principle that could save your marriage. *If you take something, you have to give something to replace it.* So if you take something away from your spouse, you must to be willing to give up something else. So, brother, don't take something away from your wife and expect her to grin and bear it—she'll only do that for a certain amount of time. For example, if you're supposed to take her to a movie and a friend reminds you of a game you'd planned to attend, don't just blow her off. Too often men tell their wives, "Baby, I know it's our time, but I have to watch the game. Just give me a few hours…" So you leave, or are glued to the television—and in the meantime, she's waiting…*frustrated.* Watch out! This is what brawls are made of.

If you promised it was *her time,* try replacing it with something else. "Honey, if you give me this afternoon to watch the game, when I come back, I'm going to take you out to a nice dinner." And be fair. If you spend $90 to $100 going to watch a football game, then take her out to eat a $20 meal, that's not balance. And she'll know it.

If you're not ready to replace something, don't take it away. As a matter of fact, don't even dialogue about it until you have the ability to replace it. If Wednesday night is your movie night, and something comes up, you need to say, "Honey, I have a proposal to work on, and it's going to take a little bit longer than I thought. We can go to the movies either on Thursday or Friday, or we can do whatever you want. You tell me, and I'll put it in my planner right now. I just have to submit this proposal by Thursday at 4:00 p.m."

She's probably going to say, "Both," because you gave her the option. Most importantly, though, the situation has become workable—because you didn't take something away without replacing it. And remember…try to replace the first thing with something of equal or better value. This way your wife will feel special, since you've upgraded your time together.

Let's look at another angle. Remember the white turtle-neck? When my wife said, "I don't like it…" I initially didn't appreciate her criticism. Yet, when I remained open to her point of view, I discovered she was right. Not only did I look better; the next day, she replaced all of them.

And then there's the story about my black Nike sweat suit. I absolutely loved it. Head to toe, I felt great whenever I wore it. Black cap, black suit, and black sneakers—*I was the Nike man*. Then Juanita looked at it one day and said, "That's a little old." Aggravated, I snapped back, "Some of your things don't look as new and fresh as this." So she continued, "Let me tell you why I don't like it." She started breaking it down…and of course, she was right.

When I bought the sweat suit, I was more than twenty pounds lighter. Really, the extra pounds shouldn't have fit into the outfit—*but it was my favorite*. I was going to wear it even if I didn't look my best. I had a hard time letting it go, so I put it in my gym locker and wore it only on the days she wasn't with me. I called it my endurance suit.

Then I took the trip to the Bahamas and ended up wearing the same clothes for a day and a half until my other ones arrived. During that trip, I decided that I wanted to work out. So I bought some new exercise gear, and when I returned she said, "Now that fits you the way it should." And I had to agree, "It sure does, doesn't it?" Then other compliments started rolling in…so I started thinking, *Yeah, I could run five more miles in this suit.* Again, *my wife's reasoning was excellent*—even if I did beat her to the punch in buying another suit. I love her so much for telling me the truth in love. And, of course, the Nike sweat suit is gone.

Learn to Embrace Flexibility

Flexibility is vital, for marriage will bring out all of your demons. For example, my wife and I were dialoguing one day and she shared that we had a lot of things to do when I arrived in New York. "All right," I said, "what time do you need me?" "I need you by 10:00." "Okay," I confirmed, "are you sure?" "Yes, I need you to be here by 10:00."

I kept confirming because I knew better—she had ministry dates on both Thursday and Friday night, and I was concerned about the extra things on her schedule. "Are you sure you want me to be there at 10:00?" I asked a third time. The truth be told, I also really wanted to work out before leaving Washington, and I could do so only between 8:00 a.m. and 8:00 p.m. If I took an early flight, it meant I couldn't exercise that morning. And later wouldn't be possible since I had a service at 6:00 p.m. A mid-afternoon workout seemed to be my only option. My mind was focused.

So I caught the 8:30 a.m. flight to arrive in New York at 9:30. When I got home, Juanita was just waking up. "Honey, I just woke up," she said. "How are you this morning?" My mind was screaming, *I could have worked out. I could have had this or that thing done…* My analytical mind started charting, and Juanita could sense my tension—so she stayed in a wonderful damage control mode. Suddenly, I turned and said, "I'm going to wash my Jeep." It really wasn't an excuse; it was an opportune time. The car hadn't been washed in a couple of weeks. Plus, I knew she needed more time to get ready.

On my way home from washing the Jeep, I picked up some coffee at Starbuck's, for symbolic reasons. I wanted her to know that no matter what, we weren't going to have an argument. I saw how the day was going and surrendered to it. *I knew I'd have to bend on this one*. We finally left the house at noon, about two hours later than originally planned. The good thing was, I'd already changed my flight to 2:30 p.m.

Juanita made a couple of extra stops before we reached our original destination…but you know what? It was worth it. When we went in, I started seeing things I liked, and she gave me time to enjoy what I was seeing. She was wonderfully flexible. My wife didn't rush me; she waited. Eventually when I said, "I'm supposed to be back at such and such time, and I can only make this flight…," we left.

Upon arriving at home, Juanita excused herself briefly to make some decisions about final fittings for the wedding, so I went up to the bedroom. As I settled in to watching the news, she came upstairs and said, "You know, honey, I really appreciate the day…" This meant a lot—because the only reason she was able to appreciate it was that I'd finally let go of making it to the gym. As much as I wanted to work out, I decided that building our relationship was more important.

I didn't realize, however, that I was about to grow again. While we were driving to the airport, she said, "Do you have time to get something to eat?" I sighed and said, "Yeah." We hadn't seen each other in two days, so she wanted to enjoy every moment we had together—even if we were running errands and taking care of marriage details.

As you've probably guessed, my wife and I have an interesting relationship—so flexibility is a must. Sometimes we see each other at the airport and say, "Hey, how are you?" Then after a quick hug, we're on our way to the next flight. "Okay, honey, you're on that plane, and I'm over here…catch you later." So for us, one meal together is special.

At the restaurant, we were talking and laughing…and she was teasing me about how I cut my chicken (instead of just picking it up with my hands). So I decided to do something different. I was in the process of cutting a really nice piece, then decided, "I'm not going to eat this. This piece of chicken is so good, I'm going to give it to her." I slowly raised my fork toward her lips. She stopped me and said, "Baby, what are you doing?" "This side is for you," I teased. "Look at how soft and tasty it is…look how much barbeque sauce is on it. This piece is for you." She took a bite, embraced me with her eyes, and said, *"You know me, don't you?"*

I learned a valuable lesson. The next time my wife asks me to fly in early on Saturday, I'm going to say, "Honey, do you remember the last time you told me to be there at 10:00 a.m.? Why don't we make it 12:30 p.m., because I have a few things I need to do." In reality, I was partly responsible because I didn't explain to her how much I wanted to work out that day. I had it in my mind, but I didn't communicate. She simply didn't understand my priority.

I also learned that I could turn a situation around and make it fun, even after struggling through difficulties. In short, I let wisdom wash my life. I embraced a situation that challenged my ego, and I learned more of my wife's language of love.

When God adds peace to you, *you're growing*. You're coming through to the other side of a struggle. That day was a big victory for me because, again, I'm a very schedule-oriented person. My day starts calculating and clicking early, and I always want to be on time. I know exactly how much I want to accomplish in a day, so I can get pretty salty when something upsets my plans.

Here's the truth: I chose to be in a relationship, so I must choose to grow as it grows. And the only way growth can happen is for me to give it a chance. In other words, I have to be flexible and change. I have to develop the ability to say, "How much time do you need?" or "Can you give me a couple more minutes?" I have to learn how to ask, "If you don't mind, could I just stop over here? I know we planned a few stops, but I just thought about this…and since we're in the neighborhood, do you have about ten minutes?"

Thinking back, that day with Juanita was one of my best, even though I was late getting back to Washington. I realized that I'd rather be a little late and *still be in love*, than to be very early and in a lot of pain. Another paradox…*but a good one*.

Hear me. If you want your marriage to survive, there are times you'll have to learn how to give and sow into your relationship. This is how God brings us into balance. It's not the quantity; *it's quality*. It's not how much your spouse does in relation to what you do. It's learning how to give, and then trusting God to do what we can't do. It's never depriving your spouse of any good thing—even if you have to sacrifice. God is faithful. He'll bless you if you'll keep listening to love. At times, it's difficult to be flexible, especially when you're used to being consistent. Yet, again, *love is a process.*

Husband, Rise to the Call

Many times when God is trying to speak with a man about his marriage, he's still arguing with the woman about the problem. And to be honest—he'd rather argue with his wife. In reality, he doesn't want to take the issue to God. Hear me, brother. If you truly understand your anointing, you won't argue with your wife. You'll keep your mouth shut and go to your heavenly Father.

God came down and walked with Adam in the cool of the evening (Genesis 3:8–9). On any one of these occasions, He could have said something like, "Adam, I know Eve is a powerful woman, so I'm just checking on you to make sure everything's okay. Do you need to talk? I know you're having some difficulties, and you need My counsel. Come on, Adam, Eve's asleep. Let's walk and talk…*come on*, just let your frustrations vent. Now listen, understand why I made her so powerful. Her heel is going to bruise the head of Satan. The lowest part of her can destroy the place of his command. So let's talk, because it's a big responsibility to cover a woman whom I made to destroy your enemy."

If Adam had any sense, he'd have gladly taken God's advice about the woman who could say a word and destroy his enemy. As long as she was happy, he wouldn't have to worry about the enemy trying to destroy their lives and legacy.

Remember, marriages are full of mistakes, and it takes mistakes to develop a marriage. If you give up the first time your spouse does something wrong, then you've already given up the ability to have power in your marriage. Light dispels darkness. Mistakes bring up unresolved issues, so each of you must develop a ministry to speak to mistakes. Otherwise, your marriage won't last.

For example, I have been saved for a long time, but I still have to keep my anger on the cross. I don't have a tomb for him yet—but one day during heated fellowship, it came to me that old pain was causing me to react. Right then and there, I made up my mind that I wasn't going to keep letting it happen. I looked my wife in the eyes and said, "Honey, I promise you…I'll never yell at you again. No matter how mad I get, I'm not going to argue." When I saw the pain in her eyes, I decided to change.

That took me back to when I said, "Teach me how to love you." Anybody can think they're in love…but only the man or woman who's taught how to love can have a healthy romance. Anybody can find a fault, but not everyone is teachable—so they can get to the other side of an issue.

Here's a reality of life: Sometimes a woman leaves a man because he's not willing to listen to love. So I embraced maturity and took control over my ability to do what was right before God. I let go of childish things and realized I was in control of me. So that day with Juanita, I thought about it and said, "Why am I yelling at my help? What's wrong with you, Wesley?" My problem was that I thought loudness equated to love. In the past, I would have said, "Well, I'm loud because I love you and I'm intense…" No! *The truth is, my loudness equated to my hurt.* My love was hurt, so I made a lot of noise.

Listen to wisdom. If you love someone only in your own way and from your own, limited experience—it may not be what he or she needs. So really, you don't have an honest relationship. And without truth, you can't have life in your marriage. If you want to build a love that lasts, ask for honest, constructive, painful, gut-wrenching, blood pressure-rising *criticism.* Once you can face the truth about yourself, you can learn to love somebody else.

Here's what God said to me: "The greatest thing you can give your wife isn't flowers, rings, money, a house, or even love...*it's growth.*" This is the best thing I can give to my wife. If she sees me changed one day, she'll love me more than flowers, money, rings, or anything else—*because I am what she needs.*

On another occasion, my wife called me and I could tell she was angry. As we talked, I realized she had every right to feel that way. I was fully at fault and 100 percent convicted. So I heard her out and said, "I understand...it's my fault, and I'm going to put some corrective measures in place so it won't happen again." Still, I knew it wasn't over. So I braced myself for a 45-minute empowerment session. I didn't say a word the whole time; I just listened until her final words were, "Honey, I love you. You know I only want the best for us."

In my silence, she knew she was getting through to me. She was assured that I was hearing her so this situation wouldn't happen again. A day later, the subject came up again, and I listened. Then I said, "I really thank you for being such a sensitive wife in allowing me to grow with you and understand how I can handle this next time. And really, you made a lot of sense. I won't ignore your wisdom, and I appreciate the way you've empowered my life. I hope you see the change that you want immediately."

Brother, there's a God *in you* that can recognize the God *in your wife*, releasing her to respond in a positive way. So rise up in your anointing and don't be bitter, harsh, or resentful. Develop the capacity to show your wife more of God than she expects you to show. Most of the time, we men show our egos instead of godliness. Wisdom says, when my wife says something out of love and concern for our common good, she's not attacking my manhood—*she wants to help us grow.*

Keep Learning How to Love

Just remember, the greatest assignment in a relationship is committing to the other person, "I'm not going to let you fail." The truth may hurt for a moment, but it will save you years of pain. Painlessness comes when you start becoming honest.

Remember the star that led wise men to Jesus. A star is composed of fire, but it never consumes itself—much like a godly marriage. Let's read Matthew 2:1–12:

> *Now when Jesus was born in Bethlehem of Judaea in the days of Herod the king, behold, there came wise men from the east to Jerusalem, saying, Where is he that is born King of the Jews? for we have seen his star in the east, and are come to worship him. When Herod the king had heard these things, he was troubled, and all Jerusalem with him. And when he had gathered all the chief priests and scribes of the people together, he demanded of them where Christ should be born. And they said unto him, In Bethlehem of Judaea: for thus it is written by the prophet, and thou Bethlehem, in the land of Juda, art not the least among the princes of Juda: for out of thee shall come*

a Governor, that shall rule my people Israel. Then Herod, when he had privily called the wise men, enquired of them diligently what time the star appeared. And he sent them to Bethlehem, and said, Go and search diligently for the young child; and when ye have found him, bring me word again, that I may come and worship him also. When they had heard the king, they departed; and, lo, the star, which they saw in the east, went before them, till it came and stood over where the young child was. When they saw the star, they rejoiced with exceeding great joy. And when they were come into the house, they saw the young child with Mary his mother, and fell down, and worshipped him: and when they had opened their treasures, they presented unto him gifts; gold, and frankincense, and myrrh. And being warned of God in a dream that they should not return to Herod, they departed into their own country another way.

When God gives new life, He doesn't promise it will be easy—*but He always sends a star.* That way, we'll look up and remember He's our source of vision, direction, and inspiration. Truth be told, the wise men traveled many miles with a heavy load to find the Savior. They left a culture that didn't know God to find something they never knew. And when they arrived in Bethlehem, these pagan men fell down and worshiped our Lord.

A star is rising in your marriage. So don't let the enemy eclipse your love. Don't let love die before it reaches its fullest potential. Open the treasure of your heart and lay it down at the feet of Jesus. Remember, you're not of this world, so you need to embrace God's wisdom for your marriage to stay alive.

Let's go back to Adam and Eve. God removed them from the Garden, but He never separated them from each other. Adam's covenant ended, but his marriage never did. From the beginning, God has always been in the process of building relationships. So, husband, walk with God and He'll help you to lead *knowing* God's plan for your marriage. And sister, stay in His presence and He'll help you to follow *believing* God in your husband.

Think about Mary. The angel came to her and said, *"...Hail, O favored one [endued with grace]! The Lord is with you! Blessed (favored of God) are you before all other women!"* (Luke 1:28 AMP). This revealed to me that Mary was favored that way because God Himself was about to cover her in perfection. Who could have known her better? Who better to cover her emotional and spiritual needs than God Himself!

And notice, *Joseph honored God.* He obeyed the Lord and took Mary as his wife. He provided for her, protected her, and didn't experience intimacy with his wife until after Jesus was born. In short, he put his own needs aside to take care of hers. Oh, yes! When a woman has a godly husband, she's definitely favored among women.

And sister, *Mary honored Joseph.* When he led them from Nazareth to Bethlehem, she followed *believing.* When God told him to go into Egypt, she followed, *believing the Lord.* And finally, when God told him to return to Nazareth, she was with him every step of the way. Hear me: The world is different today, but if you submit to your husband, *believing God,* you'll be richly rewarded.

It may not be easy, but you can still continue to grow if you stay in the Son. You can transition from pain to pleasure if you both learn to forgive every day. Then you'll enjoy the pleasure of knowing your spouse is a precious gift to your life. And you'll be able to find a divine balance in your relationship.

Learn to praise Him where you are right now, and celebrate every moment. *And remember...keep looking up.* God has a vision and purpose for you *in* and *through* your relationship. If you keep following the star, *you'll find it.*

MINISTRY INFORMATION

Bishop Thomas Weeks III
P.O. Box 60866
Washington, DC 20039

Executive Office: 202-832-1100
Fax: 202-832-8059

e-mail: executiveoffice@bishopw.com
Website: www.bishopw.com

Other Products by Thomas Weeks III

Top 10 Empowerment messages
Available on DVD, VHS, CD and Audio

Relationship Titles:

Help, Lord, I Need a Godly Man

Help, Lord, I Need a Godly Wife

Seven Steps to Releasing Your Relationship

Sisters, Don't Hurt a Brother Like That

Brother, Don't Be Crazy

Series:

The Pride Series (6-part VHS Series)

Killing the Spirit of Pride (Part 1, 2 & 3)

Pride Is Too Expensive

The Pitfalls of Pride

Don't Let Pride Become Your Prison

BOOKS: Coming Fall 2003

A Promise to Recover

Even As Your Soul Prospers

For ordering and other products information visit:
www.bishopw.com

Join *now* in partnership with the
Global Destiny Cyber Center Community
at www.GlobalDCC.com

Special Promotional subscription: Join now for only $9.95 *(limited time only!)*
Regular monthly subscription $19.95

Enjoy the viewing of live webcast from any of the five available Video on Demand (VOD) Channels!

- The GlobalDcc.com Channel
- The BishopW.com Channel
- Backtoprayer.com Channel
- Theprophetshouse.com Channel
- NDCCC.Channel

Other benefits and services include:

➢ Free TNL (Tuesday Night Live) webcast viewing of the complete service. Weekly empowerment teaching by Bishop Weeks III and Dr. Juanita Bynum Weeks.

➢ 100 plus VOD archived messages of Bishop Weeks, Dr. Bynum Weeks and other speakers

➢ 20 plus monthly Live webcast events

➢ Weekly Touch and Agree live devotional with Bishop and Dr. Weeks

➢ Sermon Notes

➢ Special Destiny Cyber Views (twice monthly)

"The Word of the Lord for your life is just one click away!"

COMING SOON
TO A CITY NEAR YOU!

Join Bishop Thomas Weeks III
as he tours the nation with the

GLOBAL DESTINY
EMPOWERMENT TOUR

For more information on the Tour Guide,
registration, or to order your
conference product package
visit us online at www.globaldestiny.com

6th Annual Global Destiny Conference

"BIRTHED OUT"

November 13 - 16, 2003

Conference Host:
**Bishop Thomas Weeks III
and Dr. Juanita Bynum Weeks**

For registration and more information visit us online
at **www.globaldcc.com**

Inspired by the book
Teach Me How To Love You

Teach Me How to Love You!

A Relationship Conference of the Decade

Host:
**Bishop Thomas Weeks III
and Dr. Juanita Bynum Weeks**

February 5 - 7, 2004
Location: To Be Announced

For more information visit us online at
www.bishopw.com